101 Cross-Stitch PATTERNS
for Every Season™

The Needlecraft Shop

101 Cross-Stitch Patterns for Every Season

CONTENTS

The Needlecraft Shop

SPRING

SUMMER

AUTUMN

WINTER

Product Development Director	ANDY ASHLEY
Publishing Services Director	ANGE VAN ARMAN
Cross-Stitch Design Manager	MARILYN SHELTON
Product Development Staff	MICKIE AKINS
	DARLA HASSELL
	SANDRA MILLER MAXFIELD
	ALICE MITCHELL
	ELIZABETH ANN WHITE
Senior Editor	NANCY HARRIS
Editor	MARYLEE KLINKHAMMER
Associate Editors	REBECCA BIRCH
	TONYA FLYNN
Book Design	GREG SMITH
Graphic Artist	DEBBY KEEL
Photographers	SCOTT CAMPBELL
	ANDY J. BURNFIELD
	TAMMY COQUAT-PAYNE
Photo Stylists	ERIN COLEY
	MARTHA COQUAT
Color Specialist	BETTY HOLMES
Production Coordinator	GLENDA CHAMBERLAIN
Chief Executive Officer	JOHN ROBINSON
Marketing Director	SCOTT MOSS
Customer Service	1-800-449-0440
Pattern Services	(903) 636-5140

CREDITS

Sincerest thanks to all the designers,
manufacturers and other professionals
whose dedication has made this book possible.

Special thanks to
Quebecor Printing Book Group, Kingsport, Tennessee

Library of Congress Cataloging-in-Publication Data
ISBN: 1-57367-113-4
First Printing: 2001
Library of Congress Catalog Card Number: 00-136221
Published and Distributed by
The Needlecraft Shop, Big Sandy, Texas 75755
Printed in the United States of America.

Visit us at **NeedlecraftShop.com**

Decorating your home for each special season has never been more fun. And creating clever gifts for loved ones has never been easier. With this collection of cross-stitch designs at your fingertips, you'll have everything you need to make every season of the year a sensational celebration.

Usher in spring with blossoming gardens made into fashion accessories and home decor accents. You'll be ready for the new baby in your family with a delightful blanket and Mother's Day will be brighter than ever with a gorgeous sachet.

Summer celebrations will be festive with ladybugs, sailboats and patriotic designs. Create a special valet box or golfer's hat and tie to present to Dad on Father's Day.

For autumn, add cats, bats and pumpkins to your Halloween decorations. Stitch a schoolhouse sampler for a gifted teacher.

Warm up to winter with hot cocoa treats and time for stitching gifts that say "I love you" for family and friends. Old-world and traditional Santas and exquisite poinsettias will make your holiday decorations complete.

Have fun stitching a project for every season of the year.

Happy Stitching

Nancy Harris, *Senior Editor*

CHAPTER ONE

Spring Sonnet

The Needlecraft Shop

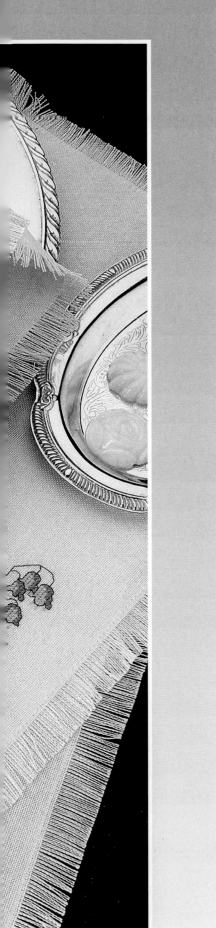

Flowers in the Kitchen

DESIGNED BY KATHLEEN HURLEY

Materials for One of Each
- Onc 12" x 18" piece (for place mat) and one 18" x 18" piece (for bread cloth) of antique white 28-count Jobelan®

Instructions
1: Center and stitch design of choice onto 12" x 18" piece and design of choice onto 18" x 18" piece of Jobelan, positioning on lower left corner 1¾" from edges, stitching over two threads and using two strands floss for Cross-Stitch and one strand floss for Backstitch and French Knot.

2: For Place Mat, stay stitch ¾" from edges; fray edges.

3: For Bread Cloth, stay stitch ¾" from edges; fray edges.

Bleeding Hearts

X	B'st	1/4x	DMC®	ANCHOR®	COLORS
	✔		#221	#897	Very Dk. Shell Pink
▨		◩	#368	#214	Lt. Pistachio Green
	✔		#436	#1045	Tan
⊙			#744	#301	Pale Yellow
◪		◩	#776	#24	Med. Pink
	✔		#890	#218	Ultra Dk. Pistachio Green
▨		◩	#899	#52	Med. Rose

Bleeding Hearts
Stitch Count:
82 wide x 82 high

Approximate Design Size:
11-count 7½" x 7½"
14-count 5⅞" x 5⅞"
16-count 5⅛" x 5⅛"
18-count 4⅝" x 4⅝"
22-count 3¾" x 3¾"
28-count over two
   threads 5⅞" x 5⅞"

Bleeding Hearts

Bluebells
Stitch Count:
80 wide x 79 high

Approximate Design Size:
11-count 7⅜" x 7¼"
14-count 5¾" x 5¾"
16-count 5" x 5"
18-count 4½" x 4⅜"
22-count 3⅝" x 3⅝"
28-count over two
  threads 5¾" x 5¾"

Bluebells

X	B'st	¼x	Fr	DMC®	ANCHOR®	COLORS
	✓			#312	#979	Very Dk. Baby Blue
■		◩		#334	#977	Med. Baby Blue
	✓		◉	#743	#302	Med. Yellow
▨		◩		#3325	#129	Lt. Baby Blue
	✓			#3345	#268	Dk. Hunter Green
▨		◩		#3348	#264	Lt. Yellow Green

Bluebells

Wild Violets

X	B'st	1/4x	DMC®	ANCHOR®	COLORS
			#368	#214	Lt. Pistachio Green
			#436	#1045	Tan
			#550	#102	Very Dk. Violet
			#553	#98	Violet
			#554	#96	Lt. Violet
			#743	#302	Med. Yellow
			#890	#218	Ultra Dk. Pistachio Green

Wild Violets
Stitch Count:
80 wide x 80 high

Approximate Design Size:
11-count 7⅜" x 7⅜"
14-count 5¾" x 5¾"
16-count 5" x 5"
18-count 4½" x 4½"
22-count 3⅝" x 3⅝"
28-count over two
  threads 5¾" x 5¾"

Wild Violets

Crafty Keeper

Designed by Mike Vickery

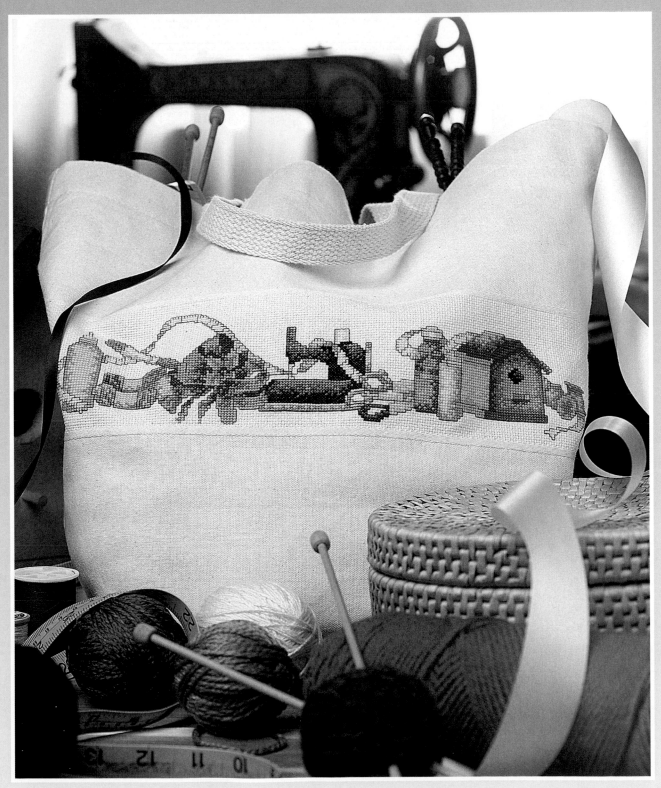

Crafty Keeper

Materials

• Tote bag with 3½" x 17" natural 14-count Aida insert

Instructions

Center and stitch design, using two strands floss for Cross-Stitch and one strand floss for Backstitch.

Stitch Count:
205 wide x 47 high

Approximate Design Size:
11-count 18⅝" x 4⅜"
14-count 14¾" x 3⅜"
16-count 12⅞" x 3"
18-count 11⅜" x 2⅝"
22-count 9⅜" x 2⅛"

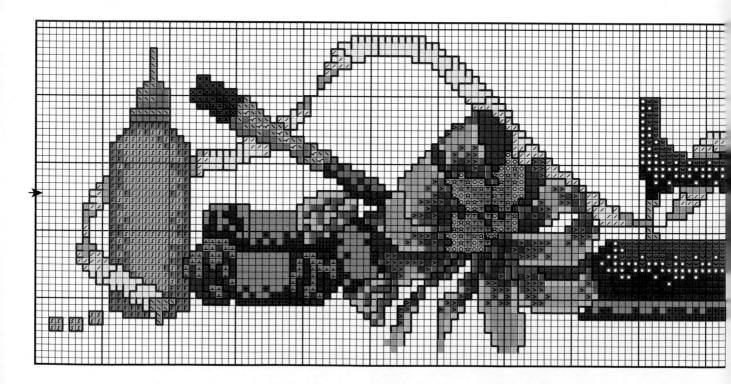

X	B'st	DMC®	ANCHOR®	COLORS
		#208	#110	Very Dk. Lavender
		#210	#108	Med. Lavender
		#310	#403	Black
		#334	#977	Med. Baby Blue
		#349	#13	Dk. Coral
>		#351	#10	Coral
		#352	#9	Lt. Coral
		#413	#401	Dk. Pewter Gray
		#414	#235	Dk. Steel Gray
		#415	#398	Pearl Gray
		#435	#1046	Very Lt. Brown
		#437	#362	Lt. Tan
X		#647	#1040	Med. Beaver Gray
T		#700	#228	Bright Green
☆		#702	#226	Kelly Green
O		#704	#256	Bright Chartreuse
／		#725	#305	Topaz
		#727	#293	Very Lt. Topaz
N		#762	#234	Very Lt. Pearl Gray
⊥		#776	#24	Med. Pink
		#783	#307	Med. Topaz
		#899	#52	Med. Rose
		#910	#229	Dk. Emerald Green
		#912	#209	Lt. Emerald Green
+		#926	#850	Med. Gray Green
		#928	#274	Very Lt. Gray Green
F		#958	#187	Dk. Seagreen
S		#964	#185	Lt. Seagreen
V		#3325	#129	Lt. Baby Blue
	／	#3799	#236	Very Dk. Pewter Gray
✓		White	#2	White

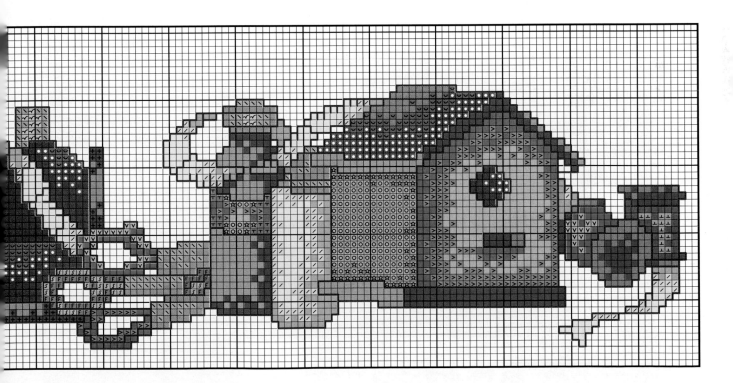

Irish at Heart

Designed by Kathleen Hurley

Materials

- 11" x 13" piece of white 14-count Aida
- Wooden tea tray with 7" x 10" design opening
- Three 6" x 6" pieces of white 14-count vinyl-Aida
- Two earring posts and backs
- ¾" pin back
- Craft glue or glue gun

Instructions

1: For Tray, center and stitch design onto 11" x 13" piece of Aida, using two strands floss for Cross-Stitch and one strand floss for Backstitch and French Knot. Position and secure design in tray following manu-facturer's instructions.

Note: For Earrings and Pin, choose motif designs of choice from graph and chart onto graph paper for proper placement.

2: For Earrings, center and stitch design of choice onto two 6" x 6" pieces of vinyl-Aida, using two strands floss for Cross-Stitch and one strand floss for Backstitch and French Knot.

3: Carefully trim one square from design edges as shown in photo. Glue one earring post to back of each design.

4: For Pin, center and stitch design of choice onto remaining 6" x 6" piece of vinyl-Aida, using two strands floss for Cross-Stitch and one strand floss for Backstitch and French Knot.

5: Carefully trim one square from design edges as shown. Glue pin back to back of design.

Stitch Count:
96 wide x 70 high

Approximate Design Size:
11-count 8¾" x 6⅜"
14-count 6⅞" x 5"
16-count 6" x 4⅜"
18-count 5⅜" x 4"
22-count 4⅜" x 3¼"

X	B'st	¼x	Fr	DMC®	ANCHOR®	COLORS
	✓			#326	#59	Very Dk. Rose
	✓			#701	#227	Lt. Green
				#704	#256	Bright Chartreuse
			●	#3326	#36	Lt. Rose
	✓			#5282	#701	Gold Metallic

Floral Coasters

Designed by Laura Kramer Doyle

Materials for One

- 9" x 9" piece of antique white 18-count Aida
- Acrylic coaster with 3¼"-round design area

Instructions

Center and stitch design of choice, using two strands floss for Cross-Stitch. Position and secure design in coaster following manufacturer's instructions.

Spring Beauty Stitch Count:
54 wide x 56 high

Approximate Design Size:
11-count 5" x 5⅛"
14-count 3⅞" x 4"
16-count 3⅜" x 3½"
18-count 3" x 3⅛"
22-count 2½" x 2⅝"

Spring Beauty

X	DMC®	ANCHOR®	COLORS
	#310	#403	Black
T	#407	#914	Dk. Desert Sand
	#550	#102	Very Dk. Violet
S	#552	#99	Med. Violet
	#632	#936	Ultra Very Dk. Desert Sand
+	#744	#301	Pale Yellow
	#762	#234	Very Lt. Pearl Gray
	#781	#309	Very Dk. Topaz
✓	#783	#307	Med. Topaz
❤	#838	#380	Very Dk. Beige Brown
	#840	#379	Med. Beige Brown
	#950	#4146	Lt. Desert Sand
	#3345	#268	Dk. Hunter Green
╱	#3347	#266	Med. Yellow Green
	#3348	#264	Lt. Yellow Green
●	#3772	#1007	Very Dk. Desert Sand
	#3823	#275	Ultra Pale Yellow
	#3839	#145	Med. Lavender Blue
	#3840	#144	Lt. Lavender Blue

Botanical Delight

X	DMC®	ANCHOR®	COLORS
✕	#554	#96	Lt. Violet
	#601	#57	Dk. Cranberry
S	#603	#62	Cranberry
	#604	#55	Lt. Cranberry
	#610	#889	Dk. Drab Brown
◐	#611	#898	Drab Brown
❤	#612	#832	Lt. Drab Brown
	#613	#831	Very Lt. Drab Brown
+	#744	#301	Pale Yellow
	#762	#234	Very Lt. Pearl Gray
	#781	#309	Very Dk. Topaz
✓	#783	#307	Med. Topaz
	#3021	#905	Very Dk. Brown Gray
	#3345	#268	Dk. Hunter Green
╱	#3347	#266	Med. Yellow Green
	#3348	#264	Lt. Yellow Green
	#3835	#872	Med. Grape

Spring Beauty

Botanical Delight

Botanical Delight Stitch Count:
48 wide x 56 high

Approximate Design Size:
11-count 4⅜" x 5⅛"
14-count 3½" x 4"
16-count 3" x 3½"
18-count 2¾" x 3⅛"
22-count 2¼" x 2⅝"

Floral Enchantment

Floral Enchantment
Stitch Count:
52 wide x 58 high

Approximate
Design Size:
11-count 4¾" x 5⅜"
14-count 3¾" x 4¼"
16-count 3¼" x 3⅝"
18-count 3" x 3¼"
22-count 2⅜" x 2⅝"

Floral Enchantment

X	DMC®	ANCHOR®	COLORS
	#341	#117	Lt. Blue Violet
	#550	#102	Very Dk. Violet
X	#552	#99	Med. Violet
S	#603	#62	Cranberry
	#762	#234	Very Lt. Pearl Gray
F	#781	#309	Very Dk. Topaz
	#783	#307	Dk. Topaz
•	#3022	#8581	Med. Brown Gray
>	#3023	#397	Lt. Brown Gray
	#3024	#900	Very Lt. Brown Gray
	#3346	#267	Hunter Green
/	#3347	#266	Med. Yellow Green
	#3348	#264	Lt. Yellow Green
	#3787	#393	Dk. Brown Gray
	#3838	#146	Dk. Lavender Blue
⌣	White	#2	White
2	Ecru	#387	Ecru

Elegant Blossoms

Elegant Blossoms
Stitch Count:
54 wide x 57 high

Approximate
Design Size:
11-count 5" x 5¼"
14-count 3⅞" x 4⅛"
16-count 3⅜" x 3⅝"
18-count 3" x 3¼"
22-count 2½" x 2⅝"

Elegant Blossoms

X	DMC®	ANCHOR®	COLORS
	#317	#400	Pewter Gray
X	#318	#399	Lt. Steel Gray
3	#415	#398	Pearl Gray
S	#603	#62	Cranberry
	#762	#234	Very Lt. Pearl Gray
	#781	#309	Very Dk. Topaz
✓	#783	#307	Med. Topaz
	#936	#269	Very Dk. Avocado Green
	#963	#73	Ultra Very Lt. Dusty Rose
	#3024	#397	Very Lt. Brown Gray
/	#3347	#266	Med. Yellow Green
	#3348	#264	Lt. Yellow Green
◇	#3716	#25	Very Lt. Dusty Rose
	#3838	#146	Dk. Lavender Blue
V	#3839	#145	Med. Lavender Blue
	#3840	#144	Lt. Lavender Blue
	White	#2	White

Floral Hoop

DESIGNED BY JO ANN EVANS

Materials

- 10" x 13" piece of antique white 14-count Aida
- 5" x 9" oval wooden hoop
- 1 yd. gathered lace
- Craft glue or glue gun

Instructions

1: Center and stitch design, using two strands floss for Cross-Stitch and one strand floss for Backstitch.

2: Center and mount design in hoop; trim edges. Glue lace to back of hoop.

Stitch Count:
95 wide x 53 high

Approximate Design Size:
11-count 8⅝" x 4⅞"
14-count 6⅞" x 3⅞"
16-count 6" x 3⅜"
18-count 5⅜" x 3"
22-count 4⅜" x 2½"

X	B'st	¼x	DMC®	ANCHOR®	COLORS
			#310	#403	Black
			#326	#59	Very Dk. Rose
			#335	#38	Rose
			#400	#351	Dk. Mahogany
			#402	#1047	Very Lt. Mahogany
			#472	#253	Ultra Lt. Avocado Green
			#725	#305	Topaz
			#727	#293	Very Lt. Topaz
			#818	#23	Baby Pink
			#3051	#681	Dk. Green Gray
O			#3326	#36	Lt. Rose
S			#3363	#262	Med. Pine Green
X			#3776	#1048	Lt. Mahogany

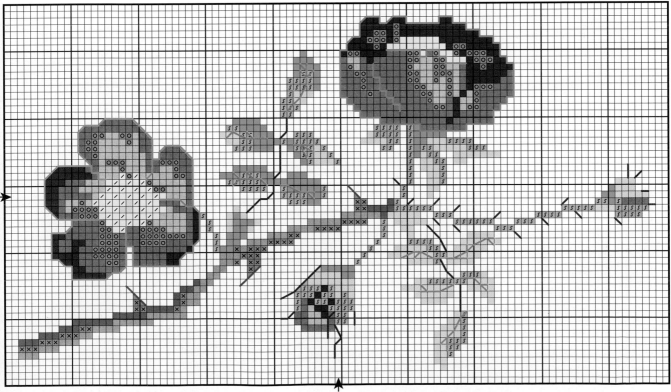

All Things Grow

DESIGNED BY TOM & FELICIA WILLIAMS

Materials
- One 6" x desired length piece and one 14" x 15" piece of forget-me-not-blue 14-count Aida
- Apron pattern (Simplicity® Daisy Kingdom® pattern No. 8236 was used)
- Hat

Instructions

1: For Pinafore, center and stitch design onto 14" x 15" piece of Aida, using two strands floss for Cross-Stitch and one strand floss for Backstitch and French Knot.

Notes: For Pinafore, follow Simplicity® Daisy Kingdom® pattern No. 8236 view "A" for materials and construction. Trim design to 7¾" x 9".

2: Center and piece design with fabric, trim following Pinafore Front No. 17 pattern piece. Construct apron following pattern instructions.

Notes: For Hat Band, choose motif designs of choice from graph and chart onto graph paper for proper placement. From fabric, cut two 2" x desired length strips and two 4" x desired length strips.

3: For Hat Band, center and stitch design of choice onto 6" x desired length piece of Aida, using two strands floss for Cross-Stitch and one strand floss for Backstitch and French Knot.

4: Trim design to 1½" x desired length. Press under ½" on long edges of each 2" x desired length strip; encase long edges of design with strips.

5: For sashes, with right sides facing, sew long edges of each 4" x desired length strip together. Turn right sides out; finish one end of each sash.

6: With right sides facing and matching unfinished edges, sew sashes to short edges of design, forming hat band. Tie hat band into a bow around hat as shown in photo.

Stitch Count:

110 wide x 128 high

Approximate Design Size:

11-count 10" x 11⅝"
14-count 7⅞" x 9¼"
16-count 6⅞" x 8"
18-count 6⅛" x 7⅛"
22-count 5" x 5⅞"

X	B'st	¼x	Fr	DMC®	ANCHOR®	COLORS
				#309	#42	Dk. Rose
				#310	#403	Black
				#335	#38	Rose
				#677	#886	Very Lt. Old Gold
				#725	#305	Topaz
				#727	#293	Very Lt. Topaz
				#754	#1012	Lt. Peach
				#762	#234	Very Lt. Pearl Gray
			●	#791	#178	Very Dk. Cornflower Blue
				#792	#941	Dk. Cornflower Blue
				#794	#175	Lt. Cornflower Blue
				#899	#52	Med. Rose
				#918	#340	Dk. Red Copper
				#921	#1003	Copper
				#986	#246	Very Dk. Forest Green
				#987	#244	Dk. Forest Green
				#989	#242	Forest Green
				#3807	#118	Cornflower Blue
				White	#2	White

Owls

DESIGNED BY MIKE VICKERY

Materials
- 13" x 16" piece of ivory 25-count Lugana®
- 1¼ yds. decorative cord
- Mounting board
- 12" x 16" wooden plaque
- Craft glue or glue gun

Instructions
1: Center and stitch design, stitching over two threads and using two strands floss for Cross-Stitch and one strand floss for Backstitch and French Knot.

Note: From mounting board, cut one 9" x 11¼" piece.

2: Center and mount design over board; glue decorative cord to outside edges of mounted design, knotting corners as you glue. Position and secure mounted design to plaque as shown in photo.

X	B'st	Fr	DMC®	ANCHOR®	COLORS
☒			#307	#289	Lemon
▽		●	#310	#403	Black
f	✎		#433	#358	Med. Brown
●			#435	#1046	Very Lt. Brown
∅			#437	#362	Lt. Tan
⊥			#644	#830	Med. Beige Gray
☑			#645	#273	Very Dk. Beaver Gray
★			#647	#1040	Med. Beaver Gray
∨			#676	#891	Lt. Old Gold
╱			#677	#886	Very Lt. Old Gold
◻			#700	#228	Bright Green
◯			#702	#226	Kelly Green
◻			#704	#256	Bright Chartreuse
◻			#725	#305	Topaz
⊤			#727	#293	Very Lt. Topaz
◼			#729	#890	Med. Old Gold
⑀			#776	#24	Med. Pink
◻			#818	#23	Baby Pink
◻			#822	#390	Lt. Beige Gray
⌂			#899	#52	Med. Rose
⌣			#3032	#903	Med. Mocha Brown
+			#3033	#391	Very Lt. Mocha Brown
◎			#3045	#888	Dk. Yellow Beige
▷			#3046	#887	Med. Yellow Beige
⬚			#3047	#852	Lt. Yellow Beige
②			#3072	#847	Very Lt. Beaver Gray
△			#3345	#268	Dk. Hunter Green
H			#3348	#264	Lt. Yellow Green
◼			#3781	#1050	Dk. Mocha Brown
	✎		#3799	#236	Very Dk. Pewter Gray
◈			White	#2	White

Stitch Count:
91 wide x 127 high

Approximate Design Size:
- 11-count 8⅜" x 11⅝"
- 14-count 6½" x 9⅛"
- 16-count 5¾" x 8"
- 18-count 5⅛" x 7⅛"
- 22-count 4⅛" x 5⅞"
- 25-count over two threads 7⅜" x 10¼"

Easter

Designed by Mike Vickery

Easter

Materials

- 10" x 19" piece of antique white 28-count Jubilee

Instructions

Center and stitch design, stitching over two threads and using two strands floss for Cross-Stitch and one strand floss for Backstitch.

X	B'st	DMC®	ANCHOR®	COLORS
■		#349	#13	Dk. Coral
●		#351	#10	Coral
		#353	#8	Peach
		#435	#1046	Very Lt. Brown
O		#437	#362	Lt. Tan
■		#644	#830	Med. Beige Gray
⌣		#725	#305	Topaz
□		#727	#293	Very Lt. Topaz
		#739	#387	Ultra Very Lt. Tan
+		#776	#24	Med. Pink
		#783	#307	Med. Topaz
Ø		#818	#23	Baby Pink
		#822	#390	Lt. Beige Gray
		#826	#161	Med. Blue
		#827	#160	Very Lt. Blue
		#899	#52	Med. Rose
		#910	#229	Dk. Emerald Green
◣		#912	#209	Lt. Emerald Green
		#954	#203	Nile Green
	◿	#3799	#236	Very Dk. Pewter Gray
T		White	#2	White

Stitch Count:
175 wide x 58 high

Approximate Design Size:
11-count 16" x 5⅜"
14-count 12½" x 4¼"
16-count 11" x 3⅝"
18-count 9¾" x 3¼"
22-count 8" x 2⅝"
28-count over two
threads 12½" x 4¼"

Teddy Bears in the Attic

DESIGNED BY BARBARA SESTOK

Materials

- 21" x 25" piece of blueberry 22-count Janina
- Four 9 mm black buttons
- Eight 7 mm black beads
- Two 6 mm black beads
- Four 3 mm black beads
- Twelve 2 mm gold beads
- 86 copper petite seed beads
- Two 3" lengths of 2 mm gold chain
- Pocket watch charm
- Heart charm
- Star charm
- Three ⁵⁄₁₆" jingle bells
- Three ribbon roses
- Ribbon bow
- 6" length of lace
- Invisible thread

Instructions

Center and stitch design, stitching over two threads and using four strands floss or two strands Broder Médicis for Cross-Stitch. Following Backstitch Instructions for placement, use two strands floss or one strand Broder Médicis for Backstitch. Use two strands floss or one strand Broder Médicis for Straight Stitch, French Knot and Lazy Daisy Stitch. Following Attachment Instructions for placement, use two strands coordinating floss for securing buttons, and one strand floss or invisible thread for securing beads, petite seed beads, chains, charms, jingle bells, ribbon roses, ribbon bow and lace.

Stitch Count:
203 wide x 160 high

**Approximate
Design Size:**
11-count 18½" x 14⅝"
14-count 14½" x 11½"
16-count 12¾" x 10"
18-count 11⅜" x 9"
22-count 9¼" x 7⅜"
22-count over two
  threads 18½" x 14⅝"

X	B'st	¼x	½x	Str	Fr	DMC®	ANCHOR®	COLORS
	✎				✎	#310	#403	Black
h						#437	#362	Lt. Tan
◣				●		#444	#290	Dk. Lemon
∪						#451	#233	Dk. Shell Gray
F						#453	#231	Lt. Shell Gray
T						#470	#267	Lt. Avocado Green
⋝						#502	#877	Blue Green
⊥						#680	#901	Dk. Old Gold
◁						#729	#890	Med. Old Gold
						#739	#387	Ultra Very Lt. Tan
	✎		✎			#796	#133	Dk. Royal Blue
S						#796	#133	Dk. Royal Blue (two strands held with)
						#797	#132	Royal Blue (two strands)
						#798	#131	Dk. Delft Blue
	✎					#829	#906	Very Dk. Golden Olive
+						#832	#888	Golden Olive (two strands held with)
						#5284		Gold Dk. Metallic (two strands)
		☐				#834	#886	Very Lt. Golden Olive (two strands held with)
						#5282	#701	Gold Metallic (two strands)
						#895	#1044	Very Dk. Hunter Green
	✎					#902	#897	Very Dk. Garnet
▷						#905	#257	Dk. Parrot Green
D			✎			#907	#255	Lt. Parrot Green
						#915	#1029	Dk. Plum
✓						#935	#861	Dk. Avocado Green
						#937	#268	Med. Avocado Green
			✎			#938	#381	Ultra Dk. Coffee Brown
	✎		✎		●	#958	#187	Dk. Seagreen
		V				#3021	#905	Very Dk. Brown Gray
H						#3078	#292	Very Lt. Golden Yellow

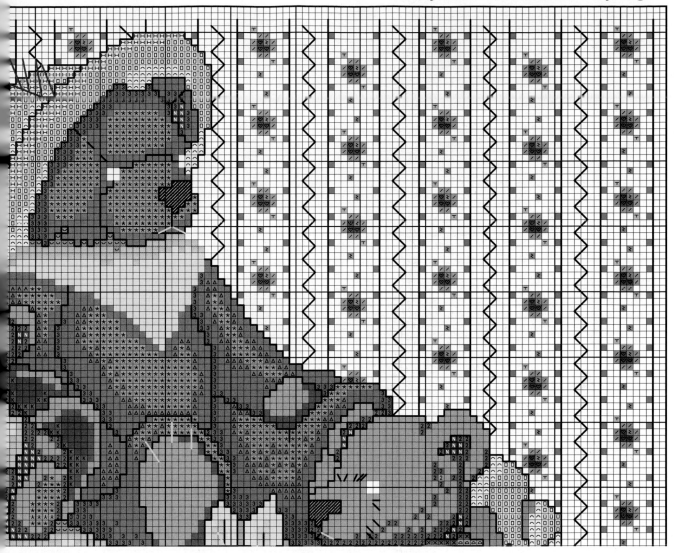

X	B'st	3/4x	Str	Fr	LzD	DMC®	ANCHOR®	COLORS
♥						#3726	#1018	Dk. Antique Mauve
◪	◪					#3727	#1016	Lt. Antique Mauve
◼	◪					#3750	#1036	Very Dk. Antique Blue
◼	◪	◪	◪		●	#3799	#236	Very Dk. Pewter Gray
✖	◪				🔋	#3804	#63	Dk. Cyclamen Pink
⬠						#3806	#76	Lt. Cyclamen Pink
⌒		◪				#3821	#305	Straw
0						#3822	3295	Lt. Straw
∅						#3829	#374	Very Dk. Old Gold
	◪					#5284		Gold Dk. Metallic
☐						White	#2	White
	◪					*#8301		Very Dk. Topaz
◼						*#8303		Dk. Straw
	◪		◪			*#8306		Very Dk. Beige Brown
N						*#8307		Drab Brown
2						*#8308		Lt. Drab Brown
▲						*#8313		Lt. Old Gold
✱						*#8314		Very Lt. Old Gold
F						*#8320		Lt. Brown
3						*#8321		Hazelnut Brown
◇						*#8322		Lt. Hazelnut Brown
						*#8504		Very Lt. Drab Brown
◼						*#8838		Ultra Very Dk. Desert Sand
K						*#8839		Very Dk. Desert Sand
◼						*#8840		Dk. Desert Sand
◼						*#8845		Golden Brown
◼						*#8846		Pale Golden Brown
	◪				●	*#8940		Tangerine

*DMC® Broder Médicis floss

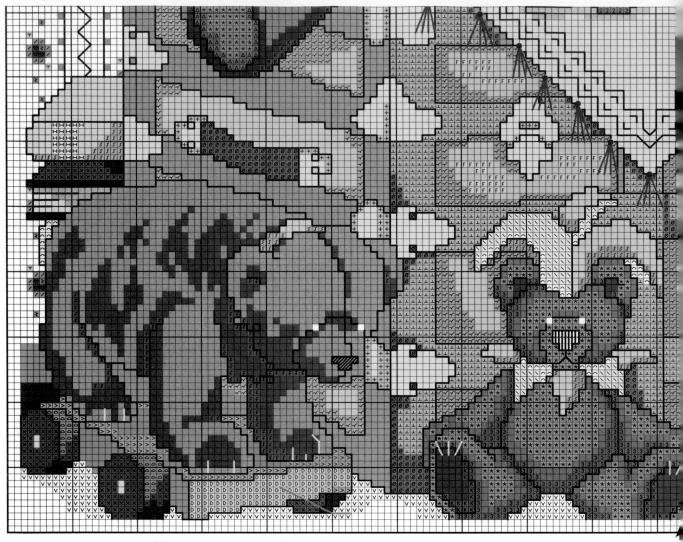

X	B'st	¼x	½x	Str	Fr	DMC®	ANCHOR®	COLORS
	✓				✓	#310	#403	Black
h						#437	#362	Lt. Tan
\					◉	#444	#290	Dk. Lemon
⌄						#451	#233	Dk. Shell Gray
						#453	#231	Lt. Shell Gray
F						#470	#267	Lt. Avocado Green
T						#502	#877	Blue Green
⟨						#680	#901	Dk. Old Gold
⊥						#729	#890	Med. Old Gold
⟨						#739	#387	Ultra Very Lt. Tan
	✓				✓	#796	#133	Dk. Royal Blue
S						#796	#133	Dk. Royal Blue (two strands held with)
						#797	#132	Royal Blue (two strands)
						#798	#131	Dk. Delft Blue
	✓					#829	#906	Very Dk. Golden Olive
+						#832	#888	Golden Olive (two strands held with)
						#5284		Gold Dk. Metallic (two strands)
						#834	#886	Very Lt. Golden Olive (two strands held with)
						#5282	#701	Gold Metallic (two strands)
						#895	#1044	Very Dk. Hunter Green
	✓					#902	#897	Very Dk. Garnet
>						#905	#257	Dk. Parrot Green
D			✓			#907	#255	Lt. Parrot Green
						#915	#1029	Dk. Plum
✓						#935	#861	Dk. Avocado Green
						#937	#268	Med. Avocado Green
			✓			#938	#381	Ultra Dk. Coffee Brown
	✓		✓		◉	#958	#187	Dk. Seagreen
		✓				#3021	#905	Very Dk. Brown Gray
H						#3078	#292	Very Lt. Golden Yellow

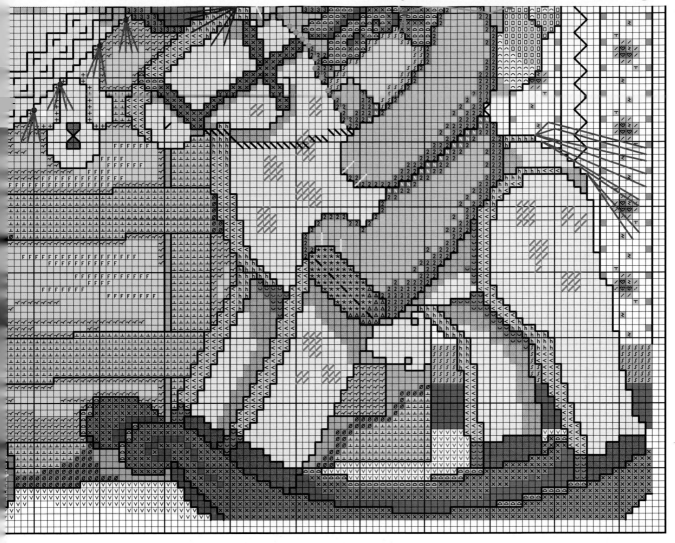

X	B'st	³/₄x	Str	Fr	LzD	DMC®	ANCHOR®	COLORS
◥						#3726	#1018	Dk. Antique Mauve
◤	◢					#3727	#1016	Lt. Antique Mauve
▨	◢					#3750	#1036	Very Dk. Antique Blue
▨	◢	◪	◢	●		#3799	#236	Very Dk. Pewter Gray
✕	◢				⧗	#3804	#63	Dk. Cyclamen Pink
◙						#3806	#76	Lt. Cyclamen Pink
⌒			◢			#3821	#305	Straw
0						#3822	3295	Lt. Straw
Ø						#3829	#374	Very Dk. Old Gold
	◢					#5284		Gold Dk. Metallic
▢						White	#2	White
	◢					*#8301		Very Dk. Topaz
▨						*#8303		Dk. Straw
	◢		▫			*#8306		Very Dk. Beige Brown
N						*#8307		Drab Brown
2						*#8308		Lt. Drab Brown
△						*#8313		Lt. Old Gold
✱						*#8314		Very Lt. Old Gold
f						*#8320		Lt. Brown
3						*#8321		Hazelnut Brown
◈						*#8322		Lt. Hazelnut Brown
▨						*#8504		Very Lt. Drab Brown
■						*#8838		Ultra Very Dk. Desert Sand
K						*#8839		Very Dk. Desert Sand
▨						*#8840		Dk. Desert Sand
▨						*#8845		Golden Brown
▨						*#8846		Pale Golden Brown
	◢			●		*#8940		Tangerine

*DMC® Broder Médicis floss

Attachment Instructions Key

- ○ 9 mm black button
- ★ 7 mm black bead
- ♥ 6 mm black bead
- ▲ 3 mm black bead
- ✳ 2 mm gold bead
- ○ Petite seed bead
- ❘ 2 mm gold chain
- ✿ Pocket watch charm
- ◆ Heart charm
- ✚ Star charm
- ❖ ⁵⁄₁₆" jingle bell
- ✕ Ribbon rose
- ✱ Ribbon bow
- ❘ Lace

☑ Backstitch Instructions

DMC®	Placement
#310	Outline of noses on Papa, Sister, Baby, Pull toy and Cowboy
#796	Blue section of Jester's hat and collar; Baby's bib; Cowboy's vest; Blue book; Pull toy collar
#829	Momma and Cowboy hats; Yellow section of Jester's hat and collar
#902	Rocking horse bridle; Rocking horse rockers; Pull toy wheels; Pink book; Cowboy's scarf
#958	Bottom and inner detail on trunk scarf
#3727	Wallpaper zigzag
#3750	Wallpaper stripes
#3799	Rocking horse; Trunk; Pull toy base; Pink book page detail
#3804	Rocking horse reins; Trunk scarf zig-zag
#5284	Front opening of Jester's hat
*#8301	Outline of footpads on Papa, Momma and Jester
*#8306	Outline and detailing on Papa, Momma, Sister, Baby, Cowboy, Jester and Pull toy

*DMC® Broder Médicis floss

Springtime Stroll

Designed by Kathleen Hurley

Springtime Stroll

Materials

- 45" x 45" piece of white 18-count Tabby Cloth

Instructions

Center and stitch design positioning on lower left cor-ner 5" from edges, stitching over two threads and using four strands floss for Cross-Stitch and two strands floss for Backstitch. Stay stitch 4" from edges. To fringe edges, see Single Fringe Illustration.

Stitch Count:
167 wide x 60 high

Approximate Design Size:
11-count 15¼" x 5½"
14-count 12" x 4⅜"
16-count 10½" x 3¾"
18-count 9⅜" x 3⅜"
22-count 7⅝" x 2¼"
18-count over two threads 18⅝" x 6¾"

X	B'st	1/4x	DMC®	ANCHOR®	COLORS
■		◢	#300	#352	Very Dk. Mahogany
■		◢	#301	#1049	Med. Mahogany
▶	◢	◢	#310	#403	Black
	✎		#326	#59	Very Dk. Rose
■		◢	#437	#362	Lt. Tan
■		◢	#720	#326	Dk. Orange Spice
■		◢	#739	#387	Ultra Very Lt. Tan
◉		◢	#740	#316	Tangerine
⑤		◢	#741	#304	Med. Tangerine
□		□	#743	#302	Med. Yellow
■		◢	#809	#130	Delft Blue
	✎		#820	#134	Very Dk. Royal Blue
	✎		#890	#218	Ultra Dk. Pistachio Green
■		◢	#910	#229	Dk. Emerald Green
□		◢	#913	#204	Med Nile Green
■		◢	#3326	#36	Lt. Rose
	✎		#3371	#382	Black Brown

Single Fringe Illustration

Unravel all threads from fabric edge to stay stitching (working each thread separately or the threads will knot). Knot groups of lengthwise threads to form fringe. Trim ends even after knotting is complete.

Welcome

Designed by Kathleen Hurley

Stitch Count:
111 wide x 59 high

Approximate Design Size:
11-count 10⅛" x 5⅜"
14-count 8" x 4¼"
16-count 7" x 3¾"
18-count 6¼" x 3⅜"
22-count 5⅛" x 2¾"

Materials
- 10" x 14" piece of light blue 14-count Aida
- Mounting board
- 1 yd. decorative trim
- 8" x 18¾" wooden hat rack
- Craft glue or glue gun

Instructions

1: Center and stitch design, using two strands floss for Cross-Stitch and Backstitch of vine tendrils. Use one strand floss for remaining Backstitch and French Knot.

Note: From mounting board, cut one 5" x 10" piece following shape of design as shown in photo.

2: Center and mount design over board. Glue decorative trim to outside edges of mounted design.

3: Position and secure mounted design to hat rack as shown.

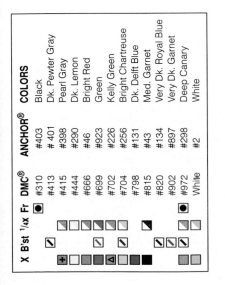

X	B'st	¼x	Fr	DMC®	ANCHOR®	COLORS
			●	#310	#403	Black
				#413	#401	Dk. Pewter Gray
				#415	#398	Pearl Gray
				#444	#290	Dk. Lemon
				#666	#46	Bright Red
				#699	#923	Green
				#702	#226	Kelly Green
				#704	#256	Bright Chartreuse
				#798	#131	Dk. Delft Blue
				#815	#43	Med. Garnet
				#820	#134	Very Dk. Royal Blue
				#902	#897	Very Dk. Garnet
			●	#972	#298	Deep Canary
				White	#2	White

Grandma's Rose

Designed by Kathleen O'Donnell

Materials

- 8" x 8" piece of pink 18-count Aida
- Porcelain jar with 3"-round design opening

Instructions

Center and stitch design, using two strands floss for Cross-Stitch. Position and secure design in jar following manufacturer's instructions.

Stitch Count:
34 wide x 33 high

Approximate Design Size:
11-count 3⅛" x 3"
14-count 2½" x 2⅜"
16-count 2⅛" x 2⅛"
18-count 2" x 1⅞"
22-count 1⅝" x 1½"

X	DMC®	ANCHOR®	COLORS
■	#326	#59	Very Dk. Rose
	#335	#38	Rose
	#420	#374	Dk. Hazelnut Brown
	#550	#102	Very Dk. Violet
+	#552	#99	Med. Violet
	#554	#96	Lt. Violet
	#727	#293	Very Lt. Topaz
	#818	#23	Baby Pink
	#904	#258	Very Dk. Parrot Green
	#906	#256	Med. Parrot Green
⊙	#3326	#36	Lt. Rose

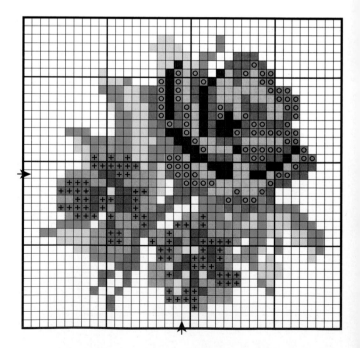

Floral Wreath

DESIGNED BY KATHLEEN HURLEY

Floral Wreath

Materials
- 20" x 20" piece of antique white 20-count Lugana®
- Footstool with 14"-round design area

Instructions
Center and stitch design, stitching over two threads and using four strands floss for Cross-Stitch and two strands floss for Backstitch and French Knot. Cover footstool following manufacturer's instructions.

Stitch Count:
102 wide x 100 high

Approximate Design Size:
11-count 9⅜" x 9⅛"
14-count 7⅜" x 7¼"
16-count 6⅜" x 6¼"
18-count 5¾" x 5⅝"
22-count 4⅝" x 4⅝"
20-count over two
 threads 10¼" x 10"

X	B'st	¼x	¾x	Fr	DMC®	ANCHOR®	COLORS
					#208	#110	Very Dk. Lavender
>					#210	#108	Med. Lavender
					#211	#342	Lt. Lavender
					#309	#42	Dk. Rose
		✓		⊙	#310	#403	Black
+					#352	#9	Lt. Coral
					#367	#217	Dk. Pistachio Green
s					#368	#214	Lt. Pistachio Green
	✓				#550	#102	Very Dk. Violet
					#742	#303	Lt. Tangerine
					#744	#301	Pale Yellow
					#754	#1012	Lt. Peach
V					#776	#24	Med. Pink
			✓		#798	#131	Dk. Delft Blue
					#809	#130	Delft Blue
	✓				#820	#134	Very Dk. Royal Blue
	✓				#890	#218	Ultra Dk. Pistachio Green
O					#899	#52	Med. Rose
	✓				#902	#897	Very Dk. Garnet
X					#973	#297	Bright Canary
T					#3347	#266	Med. Yellow Green
					#3348	#264	Lt. Yellow Green
	✓				#3853	#1003	Dk. Autumn Gold
					#3854	#1002	Med. Autumn Gold
					#3855	#301	Lt. Autumn Gold
ᴗ					#3856	#1047	Ultra Very Lt. Mahogany

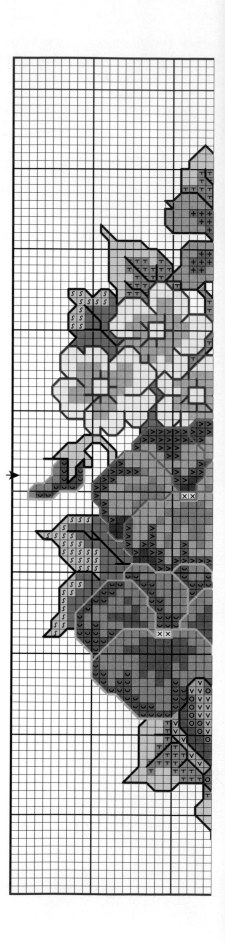

Tulips

DESIGNED BY KATHLEEN HURLEY

Materials
- 9" x 13" piece of water lily 32-count Jobelan®
- ¼ yd. fabric
- ¼ yd. lining fabric
- ⅔ yd. cord
- Batting

Instructions

1: Center and stitch design, stitching over two threads and using two strands floss for Cross-Stitch and one strand floss for Backstitch.

Notes: Trim design to 5" x 8" for front. From fabric, cut one 5" x 8" piece for back. From lining fabric, cut two 5" x 8" pieces for lining front and back. From batting, cut two 5" x 8" pieces. Use ½" seam allowance.

2: With right sides facing, sew cord to side and bottom edges of front. Baste batting to wrong side of front and back pieces. With right sides facing, sew front and back together at sides and bottom, forming eyeglass case; turn right sides out. With right sides facing, sew lining front and back together at sides and bottom.

3: With right sides facing, sew case and lining together around top edge, leaving an opening for turning. Turn right sides out; slip stitch opening closed. Topstitch around top edge of case.

Stitch Count:
52 wide x 104 high

Approximate Design Size:
11-count 4¾" x 9½"
14-count 3¾" x 7½"
16-count 3¼" x 6½"
18-count 3" x 5⅞"
22-count 2⅜" x 4¾"
32-count over two threads 3¼" x 6½"

X	B'st	DMC®	ANCHOR®	COLORS
		#208	#110	Very Dk. Lavender
S		#209	#109	Dk. Lavender
		#211	#342	Lt. Lavender
	✓	#310	#403	Black
	✓	#326	#59	Very Dk. Rose
	✓	#327	#100	Dk. Violet
		#335	#38	Rose
		#741	#304	Med. Tangerine
✓		#743	#302	Med. Yellow
		#745	#300	Lt. Pale Yellow
	✓	#780	#310	Ultra Very Dk. Topaz
		#818	#23	Baby Pink
		#932	#1033	Lt. Antique Blue
O		#3326	#36	Lt. Rose
	✓	#3345	#268	Dk. Hunter Green
		#3347	#266	Med. Yellow Green
•		#3348	#264	Lt. Yellow Green
		#3753	#1031	Ultra Very Lt. Antique Blue

Mom's Sachet

DESIGNED BY LOIS WINSTON

Materials
- 3½" x 9" piece of white 27-count Linen
- ¼ yd. gathered lace
- ½ yd. ¹⁄₁₆" satin ribbon
- Potpourri
- ½" satin ribbon rose
- Craft glue or glue gun

Instructions

1: Center and stitch design 1¼" from one short edge, stitching over two threads and using two strands floss for Cross-Stitch and one strand floss for Backstitch.

Note: Use ¼" seam allowance.

2: Fold under a ¼" hem on short edges of design; sew in place. With right sides facing, fold design in half matching hemmed edges; sew side edges together, forming sachet. Turn right side out; press.

3: Sew lace around top edge of sachet. For drawstring, beginning at center front and ¼" from top edge, weave ribbon through sachet.

4: Fill sachet with potpourri. Pull drawstring tight; tie into a bow. Glue ribbon rose to sachet as shown in photo.

Stitch Count:
33 wide x 39 high

Approximate Design Size:
11-count 3" x 3⅝"
14-count 2⅜" x 2⅞"
16-count 2⅛" x 2½"
18-count 1⅞" x 2¼"
22-count 1½" x 1⅞"
27-count over two
  threads 2½" x 3"

X	B'st	¼x	DMC®	ANCHOR®	COLORS
	✓		#312	#979	Very Dk. Baby Blue
	✓		#561	#212	Very Dk. Jade
			#601	#57	Dk. Cranberry
		◣	#827	#160	Very Lt. Blue
			#3326	#36	Lt. Rose

Chapter Two

Summer Rhapsody

The Needlecraft Shop

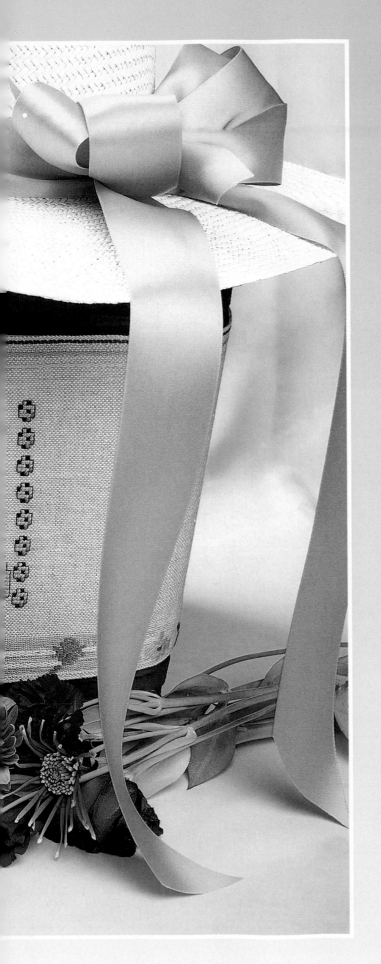

Ladybugs

DESIGNED BY
MIKE VICKERY

Materials
- Desired length of 6.9"-wide floral trellis 27-count Stitching Band
- Picnic basket

Instructions
Center and stitch design, stitching over two threads and using two strands floss for Cross-Stitch and one strand floss for Backstitch. Position and secure design to picnic basket as shown in photo.

Stitch Count:
128 wide x 56 high

**Approximate
Design Size:**
11-count 11⅝" x 5⅛"
14-count 9¼" x 4"
16-count 8" x 3½"
18-count 7⅛" x 3⅛"
22-count 5⅞" x 2⅝"
27-count over two
    threads 9½" x 4¼"

X	B'st	DMC®	ANCHOR®	COLORS
		#310	#403	Black
		#413	#401	Dk. Pewter Gray
		#414	#235	Dk. Steel Gray
		#720	#326	Dk. Orange Spice
		#721	#324	Med. Orange Spice
		#722	#323	Lt. Orange Spice
		#742	#303	Lt. Tangerine
		#744	#301	Pale Yellow
		#910	#229	Dk. Emerald Green
		#913	#204	Med. Nile Green
		#3799	#236	Very Dk. Pewter Gray
		#3825	#323	Pale Pumpkin

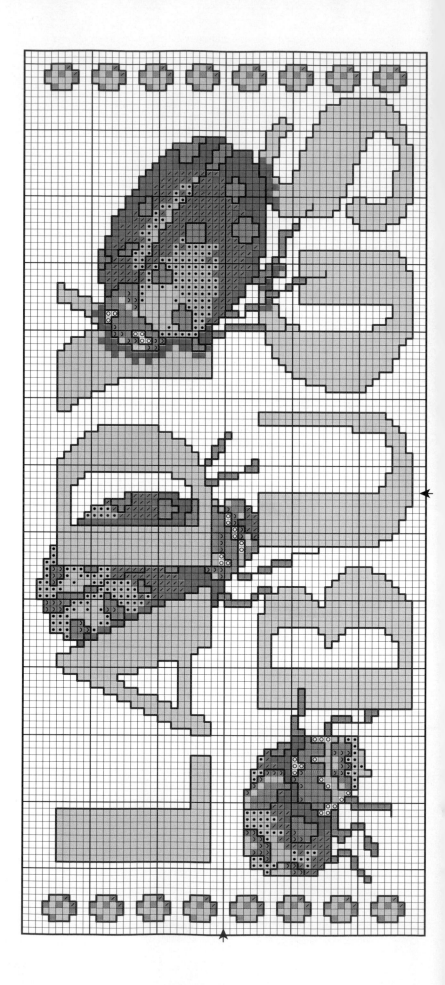

Nest for Rent

Designed by Carla Acosta

Nest for Rent

Materials

- 12" x 13" piece of white 14-count Aida
- Mounting board
- 1 yd. pleated ruffle
- 3" x 14" x 15" wooden picket shelf
- Craft glue or glue gun

Instructions

1: Center and stitch design, using two strands floss for Cross-Stitch and one strand floss for Backstitch and French Knot.

Note: From mounting board, cut one 6¾" x 7¾" piece.

2: Center and mount design over board. Glue pleated ruffle to back outside edges of mounted design. Position and secure mounted design to picket shelf as shown in photo.

X	B'st	Fr	DMC®	ANCHOR®	COLORS
∪			#347	#1025	Very Dk. Salmon
◢			#434	#310	Lt. Brown
			#561	#212	Very Dk. Jade
			#562	#210	Med. Jade
			#720	#326	Dk. Orange Spice
S			#738	#361	Very Lt. Tan
			#739	#387	Ultra Very Lt. Tan
			#930	#1035	Dk. Antique Blue
O			#931	#1034	Med. Antique Blue
			#3328	#1024	Dk. Salmon
	◢	●	#3371	#382	Black Brown
			#3752	#1032	Very Lt. Antique
T			#3820	#306	Dk. Straw
			#3822	#295	Lt. Straw

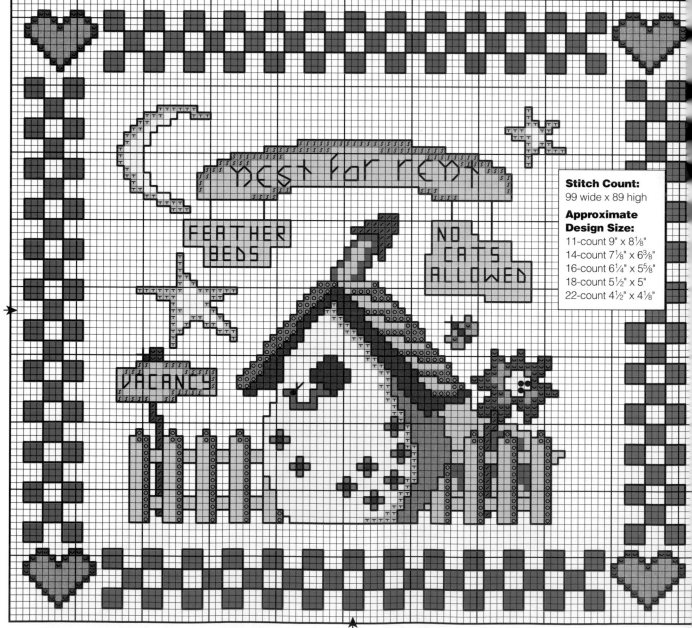

Stitch Count:
99 wide x 89 high

Approximate Design Size:
11-count 9" x 8⅛"
14-count 7⅛" x 6⅜"
16-count 6¼" x 5⅝"
18-count 5½" x 5"
22-count 4½" x 4⅛"

Let it Rain

DESIGNED BY CARLA ACOSTA

Let it Rain

Materials
• 14" x 16" piece of ivory 14-count Aida

Instructions
Center and stitch design, using two strands floss for Cross-Stitch and one strand floss for Backstitch and French Knot.

Stitch Count:
144 wide x 111 high

Approximate Design Size:
11-count 13⅛" x 10⅛"
14-count 10⅜" x 8"
16-count 9" x 7"
18-count 8" x 6¼"
22-count 6⅝" x 5⅛"

X	B'st	¼x	Fr	DMC®	ANCHOR®	COLORS
		◱		#316	#1017	Med. Antique Mauve
				#340	#118	Med. Blue Violet
				#347	#1025	Very Dk. Salmon
✗				#420	#374	Dk. Hazelnut Brown
T		◪		#434	#310	Lt. Brown
		◱		#471	#266	Very Lt. Avocado Green
				#597	#168	Turquoise
				#598	#167	Lt. Turquoise
				#741	#304	Med. Tangerine
				#743	#302	Med. Yellow
		◪		#926	#850	Med. Gray Green
O				#927	#848	Lt. Gray Green
		◱		#928	#274	Very Lt. Gray Green
╱				#931	#1034	Med. Antique Blue
N		◪		#936	#269	Very Dk. Avocado Green
				#3051	#681	Dk. Green Gray
⊥				#3052	#262	Med. Green Gray
ſ				#3328	#1024	Dk. Salmon
✚	◪	◪	●	#3371	#382	Black Brown
				#3726	#1018	Dk. Antique Mauve
				#3746	#1030	Dk. Blue Violet
		◱		#3774	#778	Very Lt. Desert Sand
V		◱		#3821	#305	Straw
⌣		◱		White	#2	White

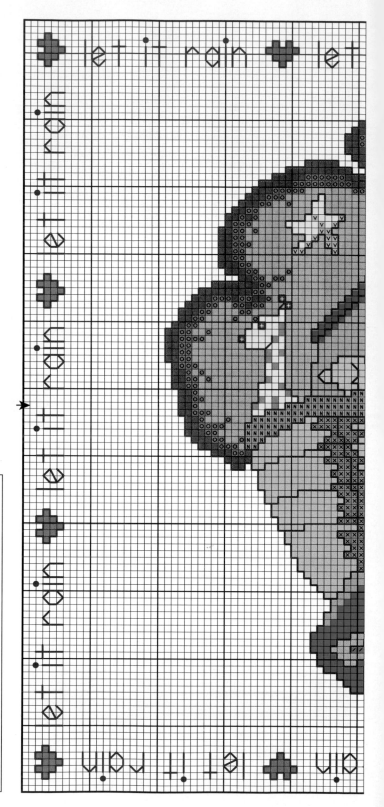

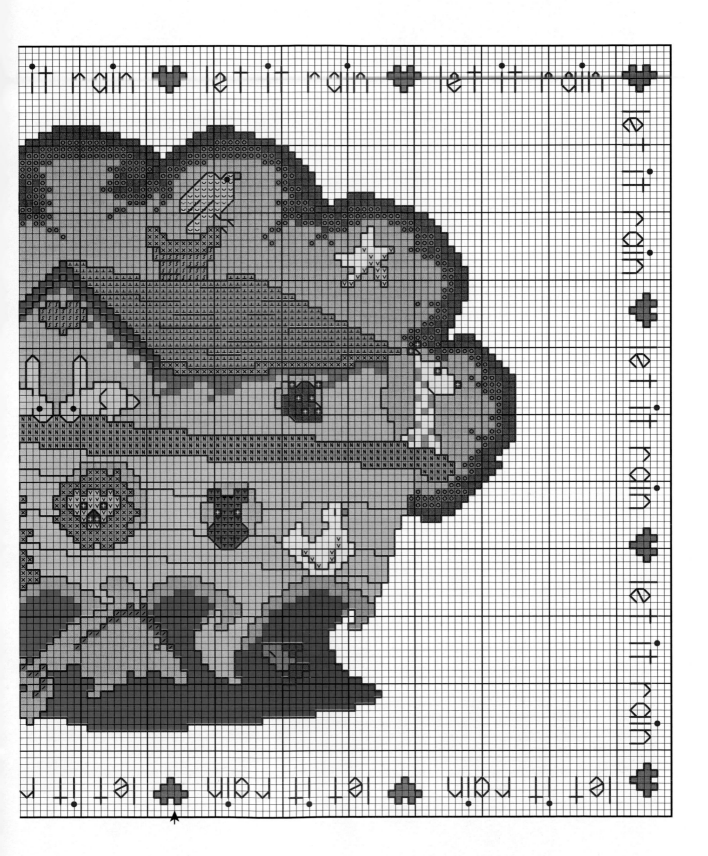

Rabbit in the Garden

DESIGNED BY CARLA ACOSTA

Rabbit in the Garden

Materials

- One 8" x 8" piece and one 11" x 17" piece of antique white 14-count Aida
- Mounting board
- 1 yd. fabric
- 1 yd. ⅛" cord
- 12" x 27" patio planter
- Felt
- 5" x 5" piece of lightweight cardboard
- 15" length of ³⁄₁₆" dowel rod
- Craft glue or glue gun

Instructions

1: Center and stitch design onto 11" x 17" piece and "Rabbit" motif design from graph onto 8" x 8" piece of Aida, using two strands floss for Cross-Stitch and one strand floss for Backstitch.

Notes: From mounting board, cut one 5½" x 11½" piece. From fabric, cut one 1" x 36" bias strip for piping.

2: Fold bias strip in half lengthwise with wrong sides facing and cord between; sew close to cord, forming piping.

3: For Patio Planter, center and mount design over board. Glue piping to back outside edges of mounted design. Position and glue mounted design to front of planter as shown in photo. Decorate planter with fabric as shown or as desired.

4: For Plant Poke, following shape of design, carefully trim around "Rabbit" design as shown. Cover lightweight cardboard with fabric. Trim covered cardboard slightly larger than design as shown. Glue covered cardboard to back of design and design to dowel rod as shown. Decorate plant poke with fabric bow as shown or as desired.

Stitch Count:
154 wide x 70 high

**Approximate
Design Size:**
11-count 14" x 6⅜"
14 count 11" x 5"
16-count 9⅝" x 4⅜"
18-count 8⅝" x 4"
22-count 7" x 3¼"

X	B'st	DMC®	ANCHOR®	COLORS
☒		#223	#895	Lt. Shell Pink
		#543	#933	Ultra Very Lt. Beige Brown
		#783	#307	Med. Topaz
		#839	#360	Dk. Beige Brown
○		#840	#379	Med. Beige Brown
S		#841	#378	Lt. Beige Brown
		#844	#1041	Ultra Dk. Beaver Gray
•		#927	#848	Lt. Gray Green
T		#928	#274	Very Lt. Gray Green
		#3051	#681	Dk. Green Gray
		#3053	#261	Green Gray
☒		#3345	#268	Dk. Hunter Green
		#3348	#264	Lt. Yellow Green
		#3354	#74	Lt. Dusty Rose
	✎	#3371	#382	Black Brown
		#3721	#896	Dk. Shell Pink
		#3768	#779	Dk. Gray Green
		#3778	#1013	Lt. Terra Cotta
		#3821	#305	Straw
		#3830	#341	Terra Cotta
⌣		White	#2	White

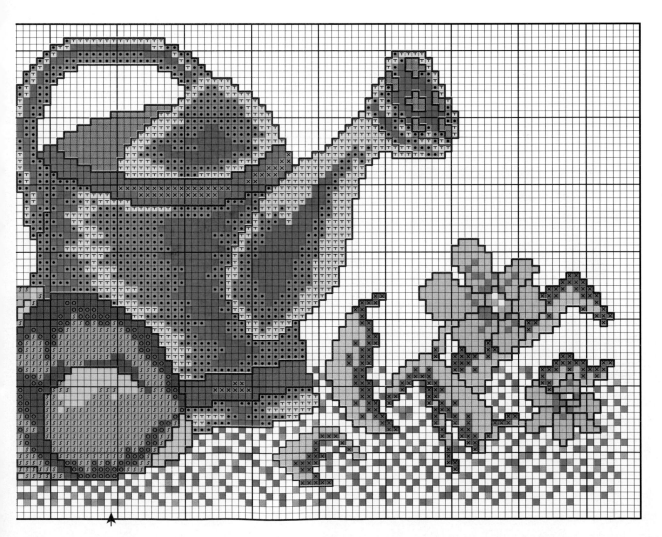

Tiger Territory

DESIGNED BY MIKE VICKERY

Materials

- 13" x 21" piece of potato 25-count Lugana®
- ¾ yd. fabric
- 1½ yds. ½" cord
- Fiberfill

Instructions

1: Center and stitch design, stitching over two threads and using two strands floss for Cross-Stitch and one strand floss for Backstitch.

Notes: Trim design to 8⅜" x 15½" for front. From fabric, cut one 8⅜" x 15½" piece for back and one 2½" x 120" strip for ruching (piecing is necessary). Use ½" seam allowance.

2: Fold ruching strip in half lengthwise with wrong sides facing. Gather unfinished edges to fit around front. Thread cord through ruching strip, forming ruched piping. With right sides facing, baste ruched piping to front.

3: With right sides facing, sew front and back together, leaving a small opening. Trim seam and turn right sides out; press. Fill with fiberfill; slip stitch opening closed.

Stitch Count:
180 wide x 92 high

Approximate Design Size:
11-count 16⅜" x 8⅜"
14-count 12⅞" x 6⅝"
16-count 11¼" x 5¾"
18-count 10" x 5⅛"
22-count 8¼" x 4¼"
25-count over two
 threads 14½" x 7⅜"

X	DMC®	ANCHOR®	COLORS	X	DMC®	ANCHOR®	COLORS
☒	#304	#1006	Med. Red	▶	#435	#1046	Very Lt. Brown
■	#310	#403	Black	N	#437	#362	Lt. Tan
▨	#317	#400	Pewter Gray	□	#543	#933	Ultra Very Lt. Beige Brown
▨	#319	#218	Very Dk. Pistachio Green	■	#644	#830	Med. Beige Gray
S	#320	#215	Med. Pistachio Green	■	#700	#228	Bright Green
+	#368	#214	Lt. Pistachio Green	2	#702	#226	Kelly Green
V	#369	#1043	Very Lt. Pistachio Green	▨	#704	#256	Bright Chartreuse
■	#433	#358	Med. Brown	◺	#720	#326	Dk. Orange Spice

X	DMC®	ANCHOR®	COLORS		X B'st	¼x	DMC®	ANCHOR®	COLORS
Ø	#722	#323	Lt. Orange Spice		T		#906	#257	Med. Parrot Green
O	#775	#128	Very Lt. Baby Blue		✓		#907	#255	Lt. Parrot Green
⊥	#822	#390	Lt. Beige Gray				#3325	#129	Lt. Baby Blue
	#839	#360	Dk. Beige Brown			◢	#3799	#236	Very Dk. Pewter Gray
•	#841	#378	Lt. Beige Brown				#3825	#323	Pale Pumpkin
⌄	#899	#52	Med. Rose			◺	White	#2	White
D	#900	#333	Dk. Burnt Orange						
△	#904	#258	Very Dk. Parrot Green						

Ming Vases

Designed by Mike Vickery

Materials

- 15" x 15" piece of antique white 25-count Dublin Linen
- Wooden table with a 8½"-square design opening

Instructions

Center and stitch design, stitching over two threads and using two strands floss for Cross-Stitch and one strand floss for Backstitch. Position and secure design in table following manufacturer's instructions.

Stitch Count:
84 wide x 72 high

Approximate Design Size:
11-count 7⅝" x 6⅝"
14-count 6" x 5¼"
16-count 5¼" x 4½"
18-count 4¾" x 4"
22-count 3⅞" x 3⅜"
25-count over two threads 6¾" x 5⅞"

X	B'st	DMC®	ANCHOR®	COLORS
◢		#211	#342	Lt. Lavender
■		#367	#217	Dk. Pistachio Green
◧		#368	#214	Lt. Pistachio Green
◻		#369	#1043	Very Lt. Pistachio Green
■		#433	#358	Med. Brown
■		#550	#102	Very Dk. Violet
▶		#644	#830	Med. Beige Gray
S		#725	#305	Topaz
◻		#727	#293	Very Lt. Topaz
◻		#775	#128	Very Lt. Baby Blue
◥		#776	#24	Med. Pink
◩		#783	#307	Med. Topaz
✕		#813	#161	Lt. Blue
✚		#818	#23	Baby Pink
◯		#822	#390	Lt. Beige Gray
◩		#824	#164	Very Dk. Blue
☑		#826	#161	Med. Blue
◡		#828	#158	Ultra Very Lt. Blue
■		#899	#52	Med. Rose
■		#931	#1034	Med. Antique Blue
V		#3752	#1032	Very Lt. Antique Blue
◨		#3753	#1031	Ultra Very Lt. Antique Blue
	◪	#3799	#236	Very Dk. Pewter Gray
◻		White	#2	White

Fruit Stand

DESIGNED BY MIKE VICKERY

Materials

- Four 8" x 8" pieces and one 11" x 14" piece of cameo peach 14-count Aida
- Wooden tray with 7" x 10" design opening
- Four wooden coasters with 3½"-square design opening

Instructions

Note: For Coasters, choose motif designs of choice from graph and chart onto graph paper for proper placement.

1: Center and stitch design onto 11" x 14" piece for Tray and design of choice onto each 8" x 8" piece of Aida for Coasters, using two strands floss for Cross-Stitch and one strand floss for Backstitch.

2: For Tray, position and secure design in tray following manufacturer's instructions.

3: For Coasters, position and secure designs in coasters following manufacturer's instructions.

Stitch Count:
110 wide x 70 high

Approximate Design Size:
11-count 10" x 6⅜"
14-count 7⅞" x 5"
16-count 6⅞" x 4⅜"
18-count 6⅛" x 4"
22-count 5" x 3¼"

X	B'st	DMC®	ANCHOR®	COLORS
		#319	#218	Very Dk. Pistachio Green
		#320	#215	Med. Pistachio Green
		#349	#13	Dk. Coral
		#351	#10	Coral
		#368	#214	Lt. Pistachio Green
		#369	#1043	Very Lt. Pistachio Green
		#435	#1046	Very Lt. Brown
		#437	#362	Lt. Tan
		#471	#266	Very Lt. Avocado Green
		#472	#253	Ultra Lt. Avocado Green
		#702	#226	Kelly Green
		#704	#256	Bright Chartreuse

X	DMC®	ANCHOR®	COLORS
	#720	#326	Dk. Orange Spice
	#722	#323	Lt. Orange Spice
	#725	#305	Topaz
	#727	#293	Very Lt. Topaz
	#739	#387	Ultra Very Lt. Tan
	#775	#128	Very Lt. Baby Blue
	#822	#390	Lt. Beige Gray
	#839	#360	Dk. Beige Brown
	#840	#379	Med. Beige Brown
	#841	#378	Lt. Beige Brown
	#842	#368	Very Lt. Beige Brown
	#904	#258	Very Dk. Parrot Green

X	B'st	DMC®	ANCHOR®	COLORS
		#906	#257	Med. Parrot Green
		#907	#255	Lt. Parrot Green
		#926	#850	Med. Gray Green
		#927	#848	Lt. Gray Green
		#928	#274	Very Lt. Gray Green
		#3021	#905	Very Dk. Brown Gray
		#3325	#129	Lt. Baby Blue
		#3768	#779	Dk. Gray Green
		#3799	#236	Very Dk. Pewter Gray
		White	#2	White

Garden Visions

Designed by Kathleen Hurley

Garden Visions

Materials

- 14" x 16" piece of white 28-count Lugana®
- 12" x 13" piece of antique white 28-count Jubilee
- Mounting board
- 1 yd. braided cord
- Wooden planter

Instructions

1: Center and stitch "Bird Bath" design onto Lugana, and "Sweet Nature" design onto Jubilee, stitching over two threads and using two strands floss for Cross-Stitch and Lazy Daisy Stitch. Use one strand floss for Backstitch and French Knot.

Note: From mounting board, cut one 6¾" x 6⅞" piece.

2: Center and mount "Sweet Nature" design over mounting board. Glue braided cord to outside edges of mounted design. Position and secure mounted design to planter as shown in photo.

Sweet Nature Stitch Count:
89 wide x 92 high

Approximate Design Size:
11-count 8⅛" x 8⅜"
14-count 6⅜" x 6⅝"
16-count 5⅝" x 5¾"
18-count 5" x 5⅛"
22-count 4⅛" x 4¼"
28-count over two threads 6⅜" x 6⅝"

Sweet Nature

X	B'st	¹/₄x	Fr	LzD	DMC®	ANCHOR®	COLORS
■	✓	◩	●		#310	#403	Black
■		◩			#433	#358	Med. Brown
✕	✓	◩			#435	#1046	Very Lt. Brown
■		◩			#437	#362	Lt. Tan
□		□	●		#444	#290	Dk. Lemon
⌄		◩			#677	#886	Very Lt. Old Gold
2		◩			#701	#227	Lt. Green
■		◩			#703	#238	Chartreuse
■		◩			#725	#305	Topaz
■					#740	#316	Tangerine
>		◩	●		#742	#303	Lt. Tangerine
■		◩			#746	#275	Off White
T		◩			#758	#882	Very Lt. Terra Cotta
■		◩			#798	#131	Dk. Delft Blue
■		◩			#809	#130	Delft Blue
	✓				#820	#134	Very Dk. Royal Blue
□					#822	#390	Lt Beige Gray
	✓			◖	#895	#1044	Very Dk. Hunter Green
O		◩			#3032	#903	Med. Mocha Brown
S		◩			#3033	#391	Very Lt. Mocha Brown
■		◩			#3347	#266	Med. Yellow Green
■		◩			#3348	#264	Lt. Yellow Green
	✓				#3371	#382	Black Brown
				◖	#3733	#75	Dusty Rose
■		◩	●		White	#2	White

Garden Visions

Bird Bath
Stitch Count:
137 wide x 106 high

Approximate Design Size:
11-count 12½" x 9⅝"
14-count 9⅞" x 7⅝"
16-count 8⅝" x 6⅝"
18-count 7⅝" x 6"
22-count 6¼" x 4⅞"
28-count over two
    threads 9⅞" x 7⅝"

Bird Bath

X	B'st	¼x	DMC®	ANCHOR®	COLORS
			#208	#110	Very Dk. Lavender
●			#209	#109	Dk. Lavender
			#211	#342	Lt. Lavender
N			#310	#403	Black
S			#350	#11	Med. Coral
\			#352	#9	Lt. Coral
			#353	#8	Peach
O			#414	#235	Dk. Steel Gray
			#415	#398	Pearl Gray
T			#420	#374	Dk. Hazelnut Brown
Ø			#422	#373	Lt. Hazelnut Brown
			#434	#310	Lt. Brown
✓			#436	#1045	Tan
⌣			#444	#290	Dk. Lemon
			#603	#62	Cranberry
			#605	#50	Very Lt. Cranberry
⌒			#704	#256	Bright Chartreuse
F			#712	#926	Cream
			#720	#326	Dk. Orange Spice
			#722	#323	Lt. Orange Spice
H			#738	#361	Very Lt. Tan
>			#783	#307	Med. Topaz
✕			#798	#131	Dk. Delft Blue
			#809	#130	Delft Blue
K			#813	#161	Lt. Blue
■			#817	#13	Very Dk. Coral Red
			#820	#134	Very Dk. Royal Blue
3			#828	#158	Ultra Very Lt. Blue
+			#972	#298	Deep Canary
♥			#992	#186	Lt. Aquamarine
			#3345	#268	Dk. Hunter Green
			#3347	#266	Med. Yellow Green
	✏		#3371	#382	Black Brown
<			#3814	#187	Aquamarine
☐	☐		White	#2	White

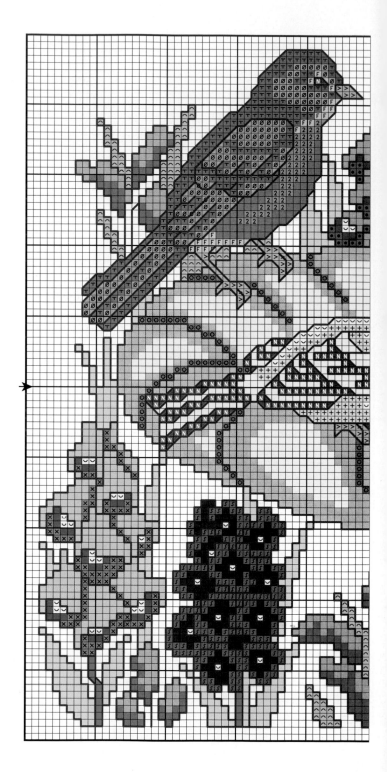

Bird Bath

Roses and Lattice

DESIGNED BY KATHLEEN HURLEY

Materials

- 45" x 58" piece of white 18-count Afghan Cloth

Instructions

Center and stitch design positioning in lower left corner as shown in photo, stitching over two threads and using four strands floss for Cross-Stitch and two strands floss for Backstitch. Stay stitch 5" from edges; fray edges.

Stitch Count:
136 wide x 138 high

Approximate Design Size:
11-count 12⅜" x 12⅝"
14-count 9¾" x 9⅞"
16-count 8½" x 8⅝"
18-count 7⅝" x 7¾"
22-count 6¼" x 6⅜"
18-count over two
  threads 15⅛" x 15⅜"

X	B'st	¼x	DMC®	ANCHOR®	COLORS
			#326	#59	Very Dk. Rose
			#335	#38	Rose
			#413	#401	Dk. Pewter Gray
			#415	#398	Pearl Gray
			#444	#290	Dk. Lemon
			#801	#359	Dk. Coffee Brown
			#818	#23	Baby Pink
			#3326	#36	Lt. Rose
			#3345	#268	Dk. Hunter Green
			#3347	#266	Med. Yellow Green
			#3348	#264	Lt. Yellow Green
			#3371	#382	Black Brown
			#3685	#1028	Very Dk. Mauve
			White	#2	White

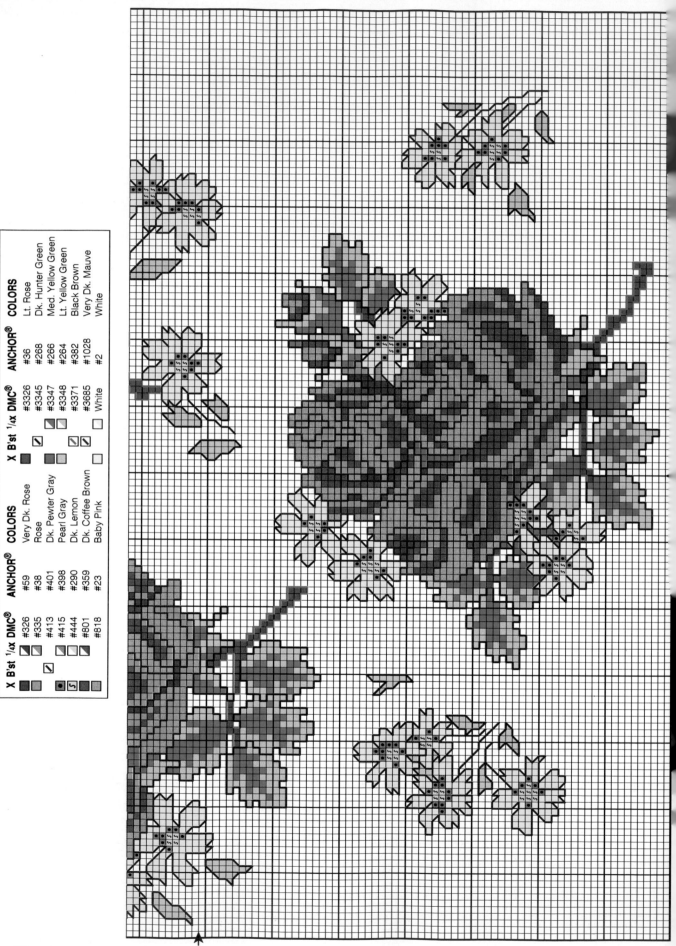

X	B'st	1/4x	DMC®	ANCHOR®	COLORS
			#326	#59	Very Dk. Rose
			#335	#38	Rose
			#413	#401	Dk. Pewter Gray
			#415	#398	Pearl Gray
			#444	#290	Dk. Lemon
			#801	#359	Dk. Coffee Brown
			#818	#23	Baby Pink

X	B'st	1/4x	DMC®	ANCHOR®	COLORS
			#3326	#36	Lt. Rose
			#3345	#268	Dk. Hunter Green
			#3347	#266	Med. Yellow Green
			#3348	#264	Lt. Yellow Green
			#3371	#382	Black Brown
			#3685	#1028	Very Dk. Mauve
			White	#2	White

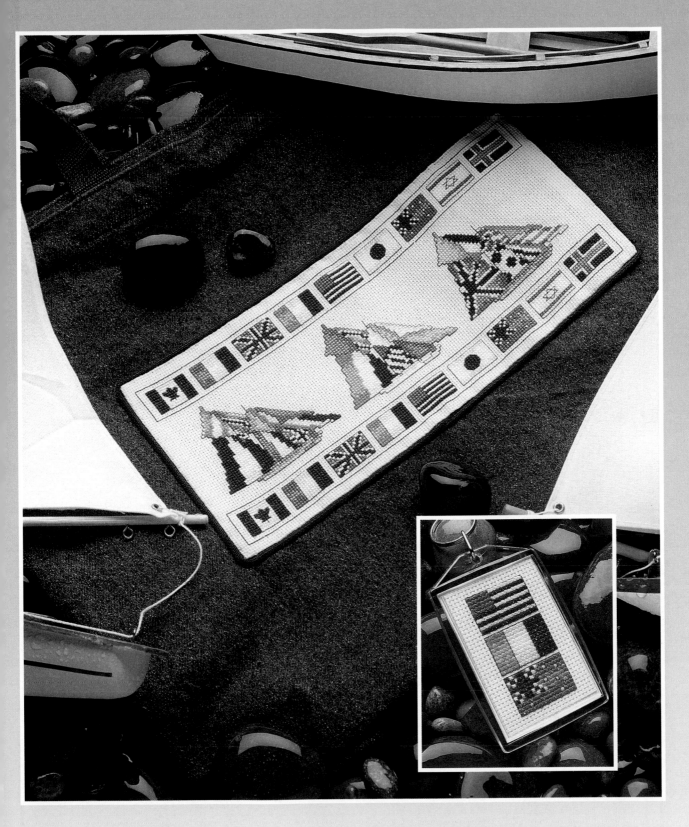

Set Sail

Designed by Mike Vickery

 Set Sail

Materials

- 11" x 17" piece of forget-me-not-blue 16-count Aida
- 1⅛ yds. braided piping
- 2" x 3" acrylic keychain with white 14-count Vinyl-Weave™ insert
- Denim tote

Instructions

Note: For Keychain, choose motif designs of choice from graph and chart onto graph paper for proper placement.

1: Center and stitch design onto Aida and design of choice onto Vinyl-Weave insert, using two strands floss for Cross-Stitch and one strand floss for Backstitch.

Note: Trim design to 5¾" x 12".

2: Press under ½" on edges of design. Sew braided piping to back outside edges of design. Position and sew design to front of tote as shown in photo.

3: For Keychain, position and secure design in keychain following manufacturer's instructions.

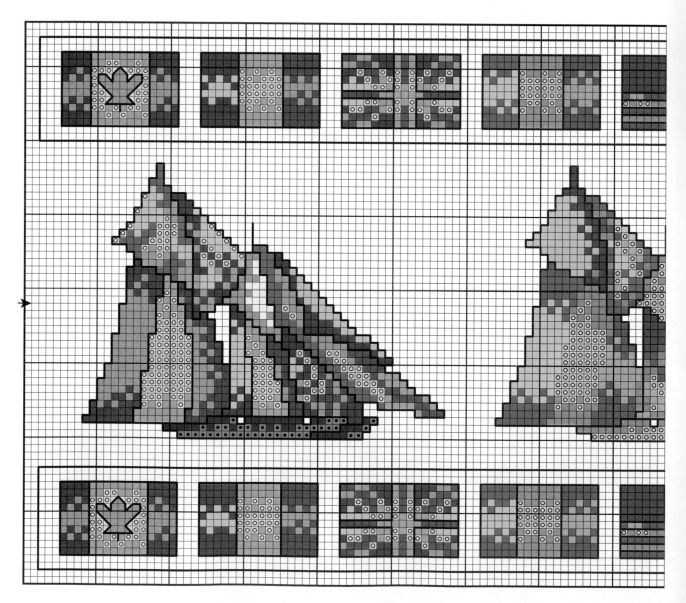

X	B'st	1/4x	DMC®	ANCHOR®	COLORS
■			#435	#1046	Very Lt. Brown
●			#437	#362	Lt. Tan
■		◪	#498	#1005	Dk. Red
■		◪	#666	#46	Bright Red
□			#725	#305	Topaz
■			#783	#307	Med. Topaz
■			#798	#131	Dk. Delft Blue
■			#799	#136	Med. Delft Blue
■			#822	#390	Lt. Beige Gray
■			#910	#229	Dk. Emerald Green
■			#912	#209	Lt. Emerald Green
	✎		#3799	#236	Very Dk. Pewter Gray
◎		□	White	#2	White

Stitch Count:
174 wide x 72 high

Approximate Design Size:
11-count 15⅞" x 6⅝"
14-count 12½" x 5¼"
16-count 10⅞" x 4½"
18-count 9¾" x 4"
22-count 8" x 3⅜"

Sunflower Bouquet

DESIGNED BY TOM & FELICIA WILLIAMS

Materials
- One 8" x 8" piece and one 11" x 15" piece of bridal white 30-count Melinda
- Porcelain box with 1½"-round design area

Instructions

1: For Dresser Scarf, center and stitch design onto 11" x 15" piece, stitching over two threads and using two strands floss for Cross-Stitch and one strand floss for Backstitch.

2: Trim design leaving 1¾" around stitched design. Stay stitch ½" from design; fray edges.

3: For Box, center and stitch "Sunflower" motif design from graph onto 8" x 8" piece of Melinda, stitching over one thread and using one strand floss for Cross-Stitch and Backstitch. Position and secure design in porcelain box following manufacturer's instructions.

Stitch Count:
126 wide x 70 high

Approximate Design Size:
11-count 11½" x 6⅜"
14-count 9" x 5"
16-count 7⅞" x 4⅜"
18-count 7" x 4"
22-count 5¾" x 3¼"
30-count over two
  threads 8½" x 4¾"

X	B'st	DMC®	ANCHOR®	COLORS
◩	◿	#310	#403	Black
◯		#550	#102	Very Dk. Violet
⋀	◺	#552	#99	Med. Violet
⊢		#553	#98	Violet
⊏		#554	#96	Lt. Violet
2		#745	#300	Lt. Pale Yellow
		#746	#275	Off White
◩		#780	#310	Ultra Very Dk. Topaz
✕		#782	#308	Dk. Topaz
•	◿	#783	#307	Med. Topaz

X	B'st	DMC®	ANCHOR®	COLORS
◼	◿	#791	#178	Very Dk. Cornflower Blue
◻		#800	#144	Pale Delft Blue
◿		#809	#130	Delft Blue
⊢		#869	#944	Very Dk. Hazelnut Brown
⊏		#972	#298	Deep Canary
		#973	#297	Bright Canary
◻	◺	#3345	#268	Dk. Hunter Green
◻		#3346	#267	Hunter Green
		#3347	#266	Med. Yellow Green
•		#3807	#118	Cornflower Blue

Patriotic Eagle

Designed by Darla Fanton

Patriotic Eagle

Materials
- 9" x 13" piece of 14-count waste canvas
- Interfacing
- Sweatshirt

Instructions

1: Position and baste interfacing to wrong side of sweatshirt; next apply waste canvas to front of sweatshirt following manufacturer's instructions. Center and stitch design, using two strands floss for Cross-Stitch.

2: Remove waste canvas after stitching following manufacturer's instructions. Trim interfacing close to stitching.

Stitch Count:
90 wide x 34 high

Approximate Design Size:
11-count 8¼" x 3⅛"
14-count 6½" x 2½"
16-count 5⅝" x 2⅛"
18-count 5" x 2"
22-count 4⅛" x 1⅝"

X	DMC®	ANCHOR®	COLORS
	#310	#403	Black
	#413	#401	Dk. Pewter Gray
	#725	#305	Topaz
	#739	#387	Ultra Very Lt. Tan
	#783	#307	Med. Topaz
	#869	#944	Very Dk. Hazelnut Brown
	#898	#360	Very Dk. Coffee Brown
	White	#2	White

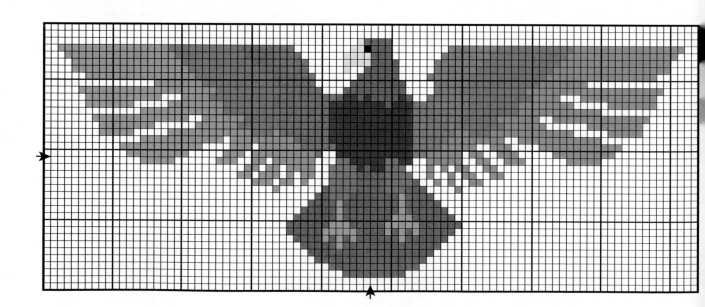

Golfer's Crest

DESIGNED BY DARLA FANTON

Golfer's Crest

Materials
- Cap with white 14-count Aida insert
- 8" x 8" piece of 14-count waste canvas
- Tie

Instructions

1: Center and stitch design onto cap insert, using two strands floss for Cross-Stitch and one strand floss for Backstitch.

2: Apply waste canvas to front of tie following manufacturer's instructions. Center and stitch design, using two strands floss for Cross-Stitch and one strand floss for Backstitch.

3: Remove waste canvas from tie after stitching following manufacturer's instructions.

Stitch Count:
29 wide x 28 high

Approximate Design Size:
11-count 2⅝" x 2⅝"
14-count 2⅛" x 2"
16-count 1⅞" x 1¾"
18-count 1⅝" x 1⅝"
22-count 1⅜" x 1⅜"

X	B'st	¾x	DMC®	ANCHOR®	COLORS
■	✔	◪	#310	#403	Black
■		◪	#452	#232	Med. Shell Gray
▫			#523	#859	Lt. Fern Green
▨			#3362	#263	Dk. Pine Green
▫			#5284		Gold Dk. Metallic

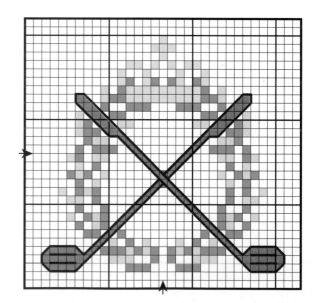

Rose Keepsake Box

Designed by Lois Winston

Rose Keepsake Box

Materials

- 10" x 10" piece of black 14-count Aida
- Wooden box with 6"-square design opening

Instructions

Center and stitch design, using two strands floss for Cross-Stitch. Position and secure design in box following manufacturer's instructions.

Stitch Count:
59 wide x 59 high

Approximate Design Size:
11-count 5⅜" x 5⅜"
14-count 4¼" x 4¼"
16-count 3¾" x 3¾"
18-count 3⅜" x 3⅜"
22-count 2¾" x 2¾"

X	DMC®	ANCHOR®	COLORS
•	#471	#266	Very Lt. Avocado Green
	#891	#35	Dk. Carnation
/	#893	#28	Lt. Carnation
	#936	#269	Very Dk. Avocado Green
	#955	#206	Lt. Nile Green
	#963	#73	Ultra Very Lt. Dusty Rose
O	#3326	#36	Lt. Rose

Flag Desk Set

DESIGNED BY JO ANNE PARKIN AND DEBBIE POPULO

Flag Desk Set

Materials

- 9" x 9" piece of white 14-count Aida
- 8" x 9" piece of white 14-count perforated paper
- Acrylic coaster with 3"-round design area
- Metallic gold floss
- Felt
- ⅜ yd. grosgrain ribbon
- Craft glue or glue gun

Instructions

1: Center and stitch "Coaster" design onto Aida and "Bookmark" design onto perforated paper, using three strands floss for Cross-Stitch and one strand floss for Straight Stitch.

2: For Coaster, position and secure "Coaster" design in acrylic coaster following manufacturer's instructions.

3: For Bookmark, trim "Bookmark" design following cutting line on graph. Overcast edges using three strands metallic gold floss. Trim felt to match design; glue to back of design. Glue ribbon to back of design as shown in photo.

Bookmark Stitch Count:
43 wide x 26 high

Approximate Design Size:
11-count 4" x 2⅜"
14-count 3⅛" x 1⅞"
16-count 2¾" x 1⅝"
18-count 2⅜" x 1½"
22-count 2" x 1¼"

Coaster Stitch Count:
38 wide x 38 high

Approximate Design Size:
11-count 3½" x 3½"
14-count 2¾" x 2¾"
16-count 2⅜" x 2⅜"
18-count 2⅛" x 2⅛"
22-count 1¾" x 1¾"

X	Str	³/₄x	DMC	ANCHOR	COLORS
■			#321	#9046	Red
■			#796	#133	Dk. Royal Blue
☐	☑	☐	#972	#298	Deep Canary
■			White	#2	White

Coaster

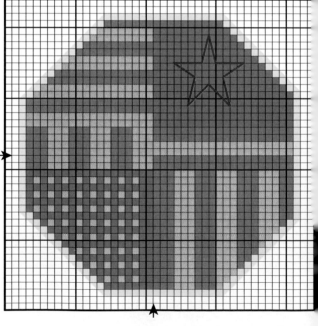

Bookmark

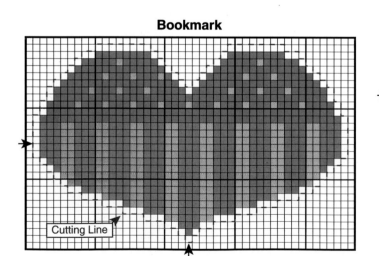

Cutting Line

Jaron's Car

Designed by Kathleen O'donnell

Jaron's Car

Materials

- 8" x 10" piece of antique 14-count Aida
- Wooden box with 3½" x 6½" design opening

Instructions

Center and stitch design, using three strands floss or two strands floss held together with one strand blending filament for Cross-Stitch. Use three strands floss for Straight Stitch and two strands floss for Backstitch. Position and secure design in box following manufacturer's instructions.

Stitch Count:
48 wide x 25 high

Approximate Design Size:
11-count 4⅜" x 2⅜"
14-count 3½" x 1⅞"
16-count 3" x 1⅝"
18-count 2¾" x 1⅜"
22-count 2¼" x 1⅛"

X	B'st	Str	DMC®	ANCHOR®	KREINIK(BF)	COLORS
●			#301	#1049		Med. Mahogany
	✓		#310	#403		Black
			#321	#9046		Red
			#400	#351		Dk. Mahogany
			#498	#1005		Dk. Red
			#699	#923		Green
			#702	#226		Kelly Green
		✓	#972	#298		Deep Canary
			#972	#298		Deep Canary held with
					#002	Gold

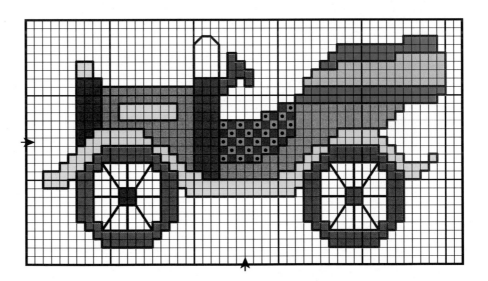

Chapter Three

Autumn Harmony

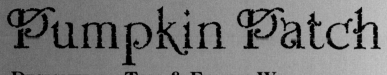

Pumpkin Patch

DESIGNED BY TOM & FELICIA WILLIAMS

Pumpkin Patch

Materials

- 14" x 17" piece of ivory 14-count Aida
- Blouse with a 1¼" x 10¼" white 14-count Aida insert
- Baby bunting with a 5" x 7" white 14-count Aida insert

Instructions

Note: For Blouse and Baby Bunting, choose motif designs of choice from graph and chart onto graph paper for proper placement.

Center and stitch design onto 14" x 17" piece of Aida for Sampler; design of choice onto blouse insert for Blouse; and design of choice onto bunting insert for Baby Bunting, using two strands floss for Cross-Stitch and one strand floss for Backstitch and French Knot.

Stitch Count:
146 wide x 107 high

Approximate Design Size:
11-count 13⅜" x 9¾"
14 count 10½" x 7¾"
16-count 9⅛" x 6¾"
18-count 8⅛" x 6"
22-count 6⅝" x 4⅞"

X	B'st	1/4x	Fr	DMC®	ANCHOR®	COLORS	X	B'st	1/4x	DMC®	ANCHOR®	COLORS
✕	◣	◪	●	#310	#403	Black	▨			#703	#238	Chartreuse
				#312	#979	Very Dk. Baby Blue	▶		◪	#725	#305	Topaz
▽		◪		#321	#9046	Red	▤		◪	#740	#316	Tangerine
		◪		#353	#8	Peach	⊥			#742	#303	Lt. Tangerine
				#433	#358	Med. Brown	●			#746	#275	Off White
		◪		#435	#1046	Very Lt. Brown	▨			#799	#136	Med. Delft Blue
�O				#437	#362	Lt. Tan	◹			#919	#340	Red Copper
				#400	#1005	Dk. Red				#917	#330	Burnt Orange
＋		◪		#677	#886	Very Lt. Old Gold	Ⓝ		◪	#948	#1011	Very Lt. Peach
				#699	#923	Green	☐		☐	#3822	#295	Lt. Straw
D				#701	#227	Lt. Green			◪	#3830	#341	Terra Cotta

old friends, like quilts, give warmth when needed

Old Quilts

Designed by Carla Acosta

Materials
- Four 10" x 10" pieces and one 15" x 18" piece of oatmeal 14-count Fiddler's Cloth
- Wooden tray with 12" x 16" design opening

Instructions
Note: For Mug Mats, choose motif designs of choice from graph and chart onto graph paper for proper placement.

1: Center and stitch design onto 15" x 18" piece for Tray and designs of choice onto each 10" x 10" piece of Fiddler's Cloth for Mug Mats, using two strands floss for Cross-Stitch and one strand floss for Backstitch.

2: For Tray, position and secure design in tray following manufacturer's instructions.

3: For Mug Mats, trim each mug mat ½" from stitched design; fray edges.

Stitch Count:
170 wide x 121 high

Approximate Design Size:
11-count 15½" x 11"
14-count 12¼" x 8¾"
16-count 10⅝" x 7⅝"
18-count 9½" x 6¾"
22-count 7¾" x 5½"

X	B'st	¼x	¾x	DMC®	ANCHOR®	COLORS
				#320	#215	Med. Pistachio Green
	◩		◩	#327	#100	Dk. Violet
				#352	#9	Lt. Coral
O				#368	#214	Lt. Pistachio Green
+		◩		#754	#1012	Lt. Peach
		◩		#799	#136	Med. Delft Blue
f				#800	#144	Pale Delft Blue
	◩			#3371	#382	Black Brown
	◩		◩	#3726	#1018	Dk. Antique Mauve
v		◩		#3727	#1016	Lt. Antique Mauve
				#3821	#305	Straw
		◩		Ecru	#387	Ecru

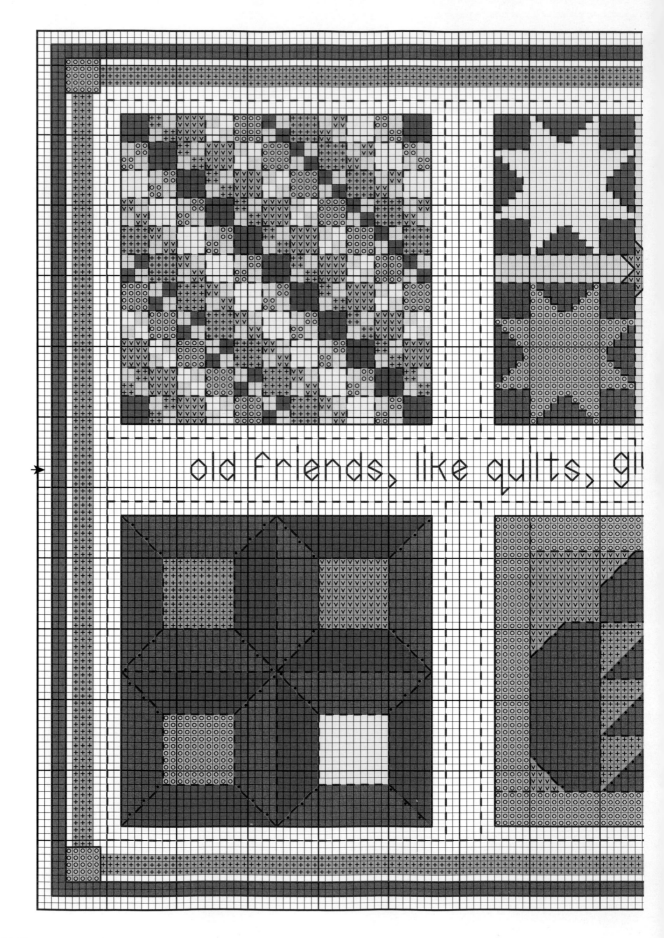

old friends, like quilts, gi

ve warmth when needed

Halloween Mugs

DESIGNED BY MIKE VICKERY

Materials for One

- Black snap-together mug with black (for "Pumpkin Gala" design) or orange (for "Spooky Silhouettes" design) 14-count Vinyl Weave™ insert

Instructions

Center and stitch design of choice onto insert, using two strands floss for Cross-Stitch and one strand floss for Backstitch. Assemble mug following manufacturer's instructions.

Pumpkin Gala Stitch Count:
127 wide x 37 high

Approximate Design Size:
11-count 11⅝" x 3⅜"
14-count 9⅛" x 2¾"
16-count 8" x 2⅜"
18-count 7⅛" x 2⅛"
22-count 5⅞" x 1¾"

Spooky Silhouettes Stitch Count:
127 wide x 29 high

Approximate Design Size:
11-count 11⅝" x 2⅝"
14-count 9⅛" x 2⅛"
16-count 8" x 1⅞"
18-count 7⅛" x 1⅝"
22-count 5⅞" x 1⅜"

X	B'st	DMC®	ANCHOR®	COLORS
		#310	#403	Black
		#367	#217	Dk. Pistachio Green
		#368	#214	Lt. Pistachio Green
		#725	#305	Topaz
		#727	#293	Very Lt. Topaz
		#822	#390	Lt. Beige Gray
		#900	#333	Dk. Burnt Orange
		#947	#330	Burnt Orange
		#972	#298	Deep Canary
		#3799	#236	Very Dk. Pewter Gray
		White	#2	White

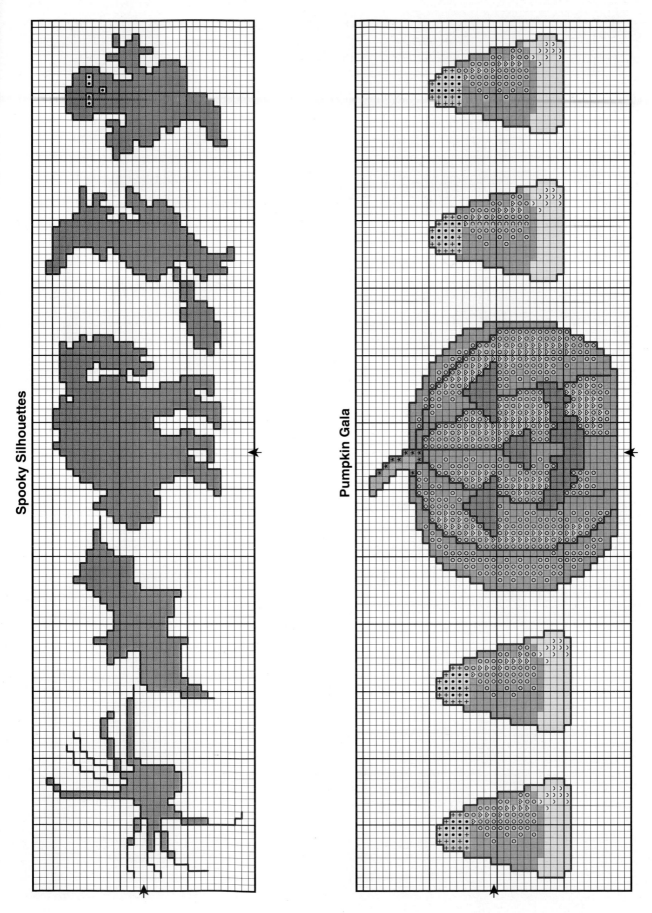

Spooky Silhouettes

Pumpkin Gala

Country-Time Towels

Designed by Mike Vickery

Materials for One
• Kitchen towel with 4½"
  x 6" ivory 14-count
  Aida insert

Instructions
Center and stitch design of choice onto insert, using two strands floss for Cross-Stitch and Backstitch of OVEN ROASTED on "Coffee" design and PURE CANE on "Sugar" design. Use one strand floss for Backstitch.

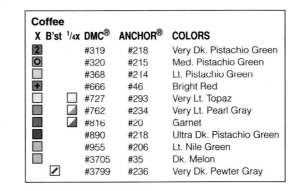

X	B'st	¼x	DMC®	ANCHOR®	COLORS
2			#319	#218	Very Dk. Pistachio Green
O			#320	#215	Med. Pistachio Green
			#368	#214	Lt. Pistachio Green
+			#666	#46	Bright Red
		▢	#727	#293	Very Lt. Topaz
		◪	#762	#234	Very Lt. Pearl Gray
		◪	#816	#20	Garnet
			#890	#218	Ultra Dk. Pistachio Green
			#955	#206	Lt. Nile Green
			#3705	#35	Dk. Melon
	◪		#3799	#236	Very Dk. Pewter Gray

Coffee

Coffee & Sugar Stitch Count:
55 wide x 75 high

Approximate Design Size:
11-count 5" x 6⅞"
14-count 4" x 5⅜"
16-count 3½" x 4¾"
18-count 3⅛" x 4¼"
22-count 2½" x 3½"

Sugar

X	B'st	1/4x	DMC®	ANCHOR®	COLORS
■			#312	#979	Very Dk. Baby Blue
▨			#318	#399	Lt. Steel Gray
O			#334	#977	Med. Baby Blue
•			#349	#13	Dk. Coral
+			#351	#10	Coral
▨			#353	#8	Peach
=			#725	#305	Topaz
□		□	#727	#293	Very Lt. Topaz
2			#762	#234	Very Lt. Pearl Gray
■		◪	#816	#20	Garnet
▨			#830	#277	Dk. Golden Olive
△			#832	#888	Golden Olive
▨			#834	#886	Very Lt. Golden Olive
▨		□	#3325	#129	Lt. Baby Blue
	◪		#3799	#236	Very Dk. Pewter Gray

Sugar

Spooked

Designed by Mike Vickery

Spooked

Materials
- 13" x 16" piece of spun silver 25-count Jobelan®
- 1⅛ yds. decorative trim
- Denim jacket

Instructions
1: Center and stitch design, using two strands floss for Cross-Stitch and Backstitch of lightning. Use one strand floss for remaining Backstitch.

Note: Trim design to 8" x 10¾".

2: Press under ½" hem on edges of design. Sew decorative trim to outside edges of design. Position and sew design to back of denim jacket as shown in photo.

Stitch Count:
85 wide x 120 high

Approximate Design Size:
11-count 7¾" x 11"
14-count 6⅛" x 8⅝"
16-count 5⅜" x 7½"
18-count 4¾" x 6¾"
22-count 3⅞" x 5½"
25-count over two threads 6⅞" x 9⅝"

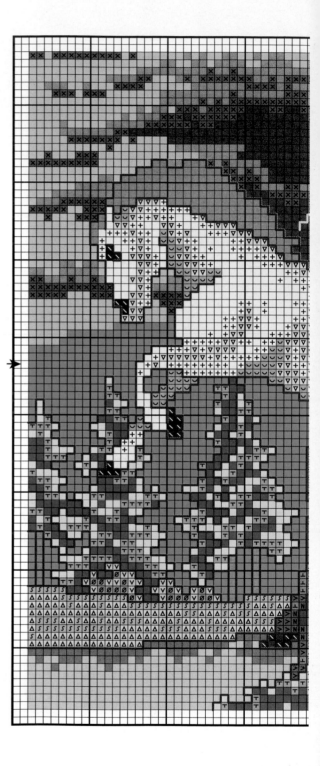

X	B'st	DMC®	ANCHOR®	COLORS
◣		#310	#403	Black
▨		#319	#218	Very Dk. Pistachio Green
T		#367	#217	Dk. Pistachio Green
▨		#368	#214	Lt. Pistachio Green
▨		#414	#235	Dk. Steel Gray
✕		#415	#398	Pearl Gray
◡		#433	#358	Med. Brown
▽		#435	#1046	Very Lt. Brown
+		#437	#362	Lt. Tan
S		#470	#267	Lt. Avocado Green
△		#472	#253	Ultra Lt. Avocado Green
▨		#543	#933	Ultra Very Lt. Beige Brown
N		#642	#392	Dk. Beige Gray
▷		#644	#830	Med. Beige Gray
ø		#702	#226	Kelly Green
V		#704	#256	Bright Chartreuse
▨		#739	#387	Ultra Very Lt. Tan
▨		#762	#234	Very Lt. Pearl Gray
⊥		#822	#390	Lt. Beige Gray
▨		#839	#360	Dk. Beige Brown
╱		#841	#378	Lt. Beige Brown
K		#842	#368	Very Lt. Beige Brown
▨		#938	#381	Ultra Dk. Coffee Brown
H		#987	#244	Dk. Forest Green
▨		#989	#242	Forest Green
▨		#3046	#887	Med. Yellow Beige
▨		#3047	#852	Lt. Yellow Beige
▨		#3790	#393	Ultra Dk. Beige Gray
	╱	#3799	#236	Very Dk. Pewter Gray
▨		#3813	#213	Lt. Blue Green
▨	╱	White	#2	White

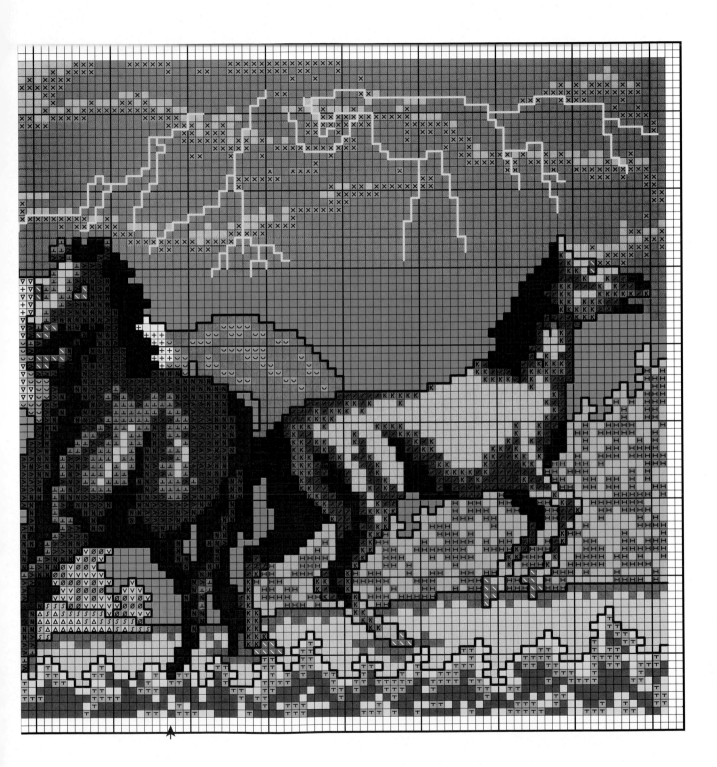

Floral Fantasy

Designed by Mike Vickery

Materials for One

- 8" x 24" piece of white 28-count Jubilee
- 1 yd. fabric
- 1½ yds. ½" trim (Entredeaux trim was used on projects shown)

Instructions

Note: Select color key of choice.

1: Center and stitch left half of design, stitching over two threads and using two strands floss for Cross-Stitch and one strand floss for Backstitch. Continue right half of design by repeating in reverse order, leaving four threads between halves.

Notes: Trim design to 4" x 20½" for center. From fabric, cut one 7" x 20½" piece for top edge, one 20½" x 24½" piece for bottom and one 20½" x 33½" piece for pillowcase back. Cut trim in half. Use ½" seam allowance.

2: Fold top edge piece in half with wrong sides facing; press. With right sides facing, sew top edge, center, bottom and trim pieces together according to Front Assembly Diagram, forming pillowcase front.

3: Fold under 3" on one 20½" edge of pillowcase back; press. Matching folded edges and with right sides facing, sew pillowcase front and back together at sides and bottom; turn right sides out. Top stitch around top edge and back of pillowcase as indicated on Front Assembly Diagram.

Blue Flowers			
X	B'st	DMC®	ANCHOR®	COLORS
■		#312	#979	Very Dk. Baby Blue
■		#319	#218	Very Dk. Pistachio Green
■		#320	#215	Mec. Pistachio Green
O		#334	#977	Mec. Baby Blue
+		#368	#214	Lt. Pistachio Green
		#725	#305	Topez
		#775	#128	Very Lt. Baby Blue
		#3325	#129	Lt. Eaby Blue
	◣	#3799	#236	Very Dk. Pewter Gray

Yellow Flowers			
X	B'st	DMC®	ANCHOR®	COLORS
■		#319	#218	Very Dk. Pistachio Green
■		#320	#215	Med. Pistachio Green
O		#368	#214	Lt. Pistachio Green
		#725	#305	Topaz
		#744	#301	Pale Yellow
■		#745	#300	Lt. Pale Yellow
■		#3799	#236	Very Dk. Pewter Gray
+		#3823	#275	Ultra Pale Yellow
		White	#2	White

Front Assembly Diagram

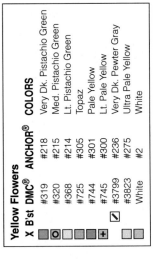

Bottom

Trim — Center — Trim — Topstitch

Top Edge

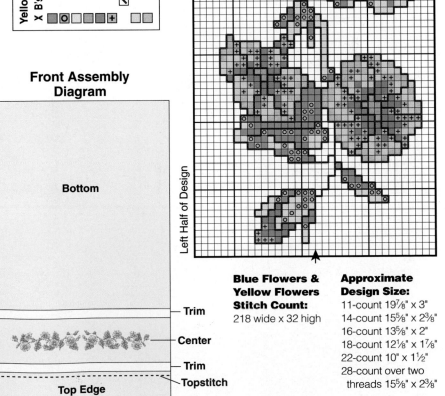

Left Half of Design

Blue Flowers & Yellow Flowers Stitch Count:
218 wide x 32 high

Approximate Design Size:
11-count 19⅞" x 3"
14-count 15⅝" x 2⅜"
16-count 13⅝" x 2"
18-count 12⅛" x 1⅞"
22-count 10" x 1½"
28-count over two threads 15⅝" x 2⅜"

Home on the Farm

Designed by Mike Vickery

Materials
- 10" x 20" piece of antique white 28-count Cashel Linen®
- Mounting board
- 1¼ yds. twisted cord
- Wooden wall decor with 5" x 19" design area
- Craft glue or glue gun

Instructions
1: Center and stitch design, stitching over two threads and using two strands floss for Cross-Stitch and one strand floss for Backstitch.

Note: From mounting board, cut one 4½" x 14½" piece.

2: Center and mount design over board. Glue twisted cord to outside edges of mounted design. Position and secure mounted design to wall decor as shown in photo.

Stitch Count:
200 wide x 60 high

**Approximate
Design Size:**
11-count 18¼" x 5½"
14-count 14⅜" x 4⅜"
16-count 12½" x 3¾"
18-count 11⅛" x 3⅜"
22-count 9⅛" x 2¾"
28-count over two
   threads 14⅜" x 4⅜"

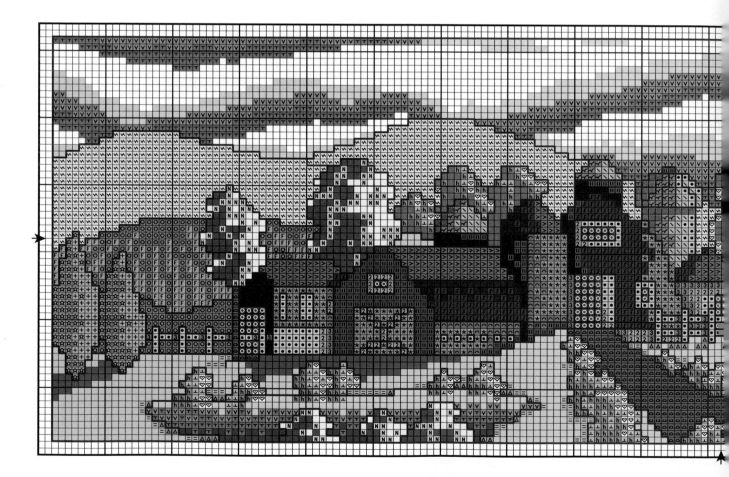

X	DMC®	ANCHOR®	COLORS		X B'st	DMC®	ANCHOR®	COLORS
	#301	#1049	Med. Mahogany			#775	#128	Very Lt. Baby Blue
	#310	#403	Black			#783	#307	Med. Topaz
	#317	#400	Pewter Gray			#814	#45	Dk. Garnet
	#319	#218	Very Dk. Pistachio Green		2	#822	#390	Lt. Beige Gray
	#334	#977	Med. Baby Blue			#900	#333	Dk. Burnt Orange
	#402	#1047	Very Lt. Mahogany		h	#971	#316	Pumpkin
	#415	#398	Pearl Gray			#973	#297	Bright Canary
	#433	#358	Med. Brown			#986	#246	Very Dk. Forest Green
	#437	#362	Lt. Tan			#988	#243	Med. Forest Green
	#445	#288	Lt. Lemon		V	#3325	#129	Lt. Baby Blue
3	#644	#830	Med. Beige Gray			#3705	#35	Dk. Melon
	#666	#46	Bright Red			#3706	#33	Med. Melon
	#700	#228	Bright Green		T	#3755	#140	Baby Blue
	#702	#226	Kelly Green			#3776	#1048	Lt. Mahogany
	#704	#256	Bright Chartreuse			#3799	#236	Very Dk. Pewter Gray
N	#725	#305	Topaz		F	#3820	#306	Dk. Straw
	#727	#293	Very Lt. Topaz		O	#3822	#295	Lt. Straw
	#762	#234	Very Lt. Pearl Gray		•	White	#2	White
	#772	#259	Very Lt. Yellow Green					

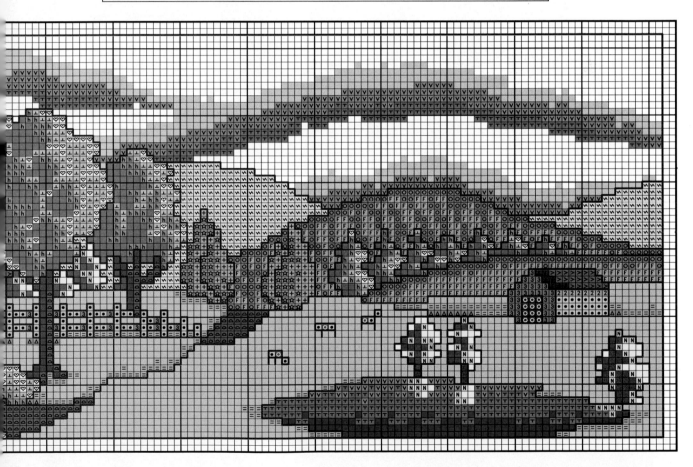

Welcome Guest

DESIGNED BY HOPE MURPHY

Materials
- 17" x 37" piece of seacrest green 14-count Rustico Aida®
- ½ yd. fabric

Instructions
1: Center and stitch design onto each corner positioning 1" from edges, using two strands floss for Cross-Stitch and Straight Stitch. Use one strand floss or one strand 4 mm ribbon for Backstitch. Repeat border design between corner motifs.

Notes: From fabric, cut one 17" x 37" piece for back. Use ½" seam allowance.

2: With right sides facing, sew design and back together, leaving an opening for turning. Turn right sides out; press. Slip stitch opening closed.

One Motif (excluding repeated border) Stitch Count:
52 wide x 52 high

Approximate Design Size:
11-count 4¾" x 4¾"
14-count 3¾" x 3¾"
16-count 3¼" x 3¼"
18-count 3" x 3"
22-count 2⅜" x 2⅜"

X	B'st	Str	DMC®	ANCHOR®	BUCILLA®(4 mm)	COLORS
▨	✓		#367	#217		Dk. Pistachio Green
	✓	✓	#433	#358		Med. Brown
▨	✓		#520	#862		Dk. Fern Green
▨			#783	#307		Med. Topaz
▨	✓		#890	#218		Ultra Dk. Pistachio Green
	✓				#511	Sunset

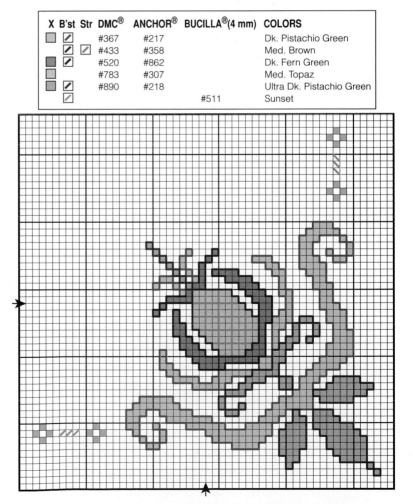

Room for Love

DESIGNED BY CHRISTINE A. HENDRICKS

Materials
- 11" x 13" piece of ivory 14-count Aida
- 12 cm bell pull

Instructions

1: Center and stitch design, using two strands floss for Cross-Stitch and one strand floss for Back-stitch and French Knot.

Note: Trim design to 5½" x 10".

2: Fold under a ½" hem on side edges; sew in place. Fold under a 1" hem on top and bottom edges; slip stitch in place. Insert bell pull into top and bottom edges following manufacturer's instructions.

Stitch Count:
63 wide x 99 high

Approximate Design Size:
11-count 5¾" x 9"
14-count 4½" x 7⅛"
16-count 4" x 6¼"
18-count 3½" x 5½"
22-count 2⅞" x 4½"

X	¼x	ANCHOR®	DMC®	COLORS	X B'st	¼x	Fr	ANCHOR®	DMC®	COLORS
		#38	#335	Blossom Pink Med.	h			#307	#783	Topaz Med.
T		#42	#309	Carmine Rose Med.	>			#326	#720	Apricot Dk.
O		#52	#899	China Rose Med. Dk.			●	#382	#3371	Fudge Dk.
f		#255	#907	Parrot Green Med. Lt.				#388	#842	Ecru Med.
		#256	#906	Parrot Green Med.	2			#933	#543	Fawn Vy. Lt.
		#289	#307	Canary Yellow Med. Lt.				#1009	#3770	Copper Vy. Lt.
V		#290	#444	Canary Yellow Med.				#1032	#3752	Antique Blue Vy. Lt.
=		#302	#743	Citrus Med. Lt.	+			#1034	#931	Antique Blue Med.
		#303	#742	Citrus Med.				#1035	#930	Antique Blue Dk.

Gentleman Golfer

Designed by Darla Fanton

Materials

- 12" x 17" piece of 10-count waste canvas
- Sweater
- Interfacing

Instructions

1: Position and baste interfacing to wrong side of sweater; next apply waste canvas to front of sweater following manufacturer's instructions. Center and stitch design, using four strands floss for Cross-Stitch and two strands floss for Backstitch.

2: Remove waste canvas after stitching following manufacturer's instructions. Trim interfacing close to stitching.

Stitch Count:
55 wide x 113 high

Approximate Design Size:
10-count 5½" x 11⅜"
11-count 5" x 10⅜"
14-count 4" x 8⅛"
16-count 3½" x 7⅛"
18-count 3⅛" x 6⅜"
22-count 2½" x 5⅛"

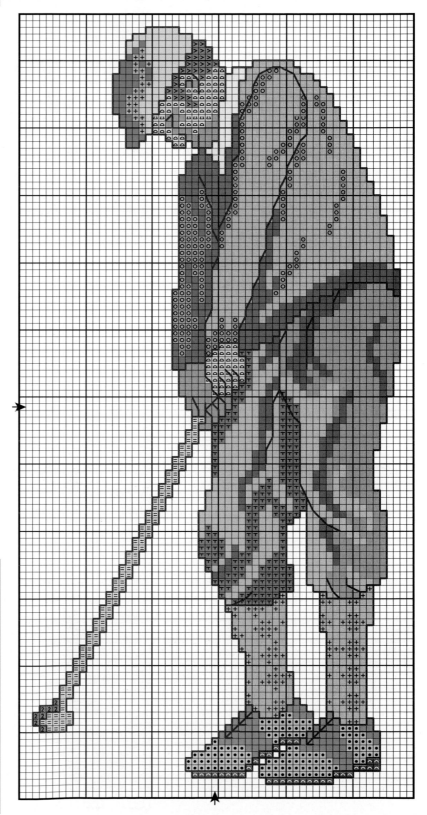

X	B'st	DMC®	ANCHOR®	COLORS
		#321	#9046	Red
		#407	#914	Dk. Desert Sand
		#434	#310	Lt. Brown
		#435	#1046	Very Lt. Brown
		#437	#362	Lt. Tan
		#498	#1005	Dk. Red
		#632	#936	Ultra Very Dk. Desert Sand
		#739	#387	Ultra Very Lt. Tan
		#754	#1012	Lt. Peach
		#801	#359	Dk. Coffee Brown
		#815	#43	Med. Garnet
		#840	#379	Med. Beige Brown
	✓	#938	#381	Ultra Dk. Coffee Brown
		#948	#1011	Very Lt. Peach
		#3051	#681	Dk. Green Gray
		#3052	#262	Med. Green Gray
		#3053	#261	Green Gray
		#3064	#883	Desert Sand
		Ecru	#387	Ecru

Sunflower

Designed by Laura Kramer Doyle

Materials
- Suede cloth purse with a 4¾" x 7" white 14-count Aida insert

Instructions
Center and stitch design, using three strands floss for Cross-Stitch.

Stitch Count:
58 wide x 78 high

Approximate Design Size:
11-count 5⅜" x 7⅛"
14-count 4¼" x 5⅝"
16-count 3⅝" x 4⅞"
18-count 3¼" x 4⅜"
22-count 2⅝" x 3⅝"

X	DMC®	ANCHOR®	COLORS
◘	#300	#352	Very Dk. Mahogany
	#301	#1049	Med. Mahogany
	#433	#358	Med. Brown
+	#725	#305	Topaz
	#727	#293	Very Lt. Topaz
	#781	#309	Very Dk. Topaz
•	#783	#307	Med. Topaz
2	#890	#218	Ultra Dk. Pistachio Green
	#938	#381	Ultra Dk. Coffee Brown
	#3345	#268	Dk. Hunter Green
=	#3347	#266	Med. Yellow Green
	#3348	#264	Lt. Yellow Green

Haunted House

DESIGNED BY MIKE VICKERY

Haunted House

Materials

- 15" x 15" piece of orange 14-count Aida
- Basket
- Desired amount of fabric
- Mounting board
- 1¼ yds. ⅛" cord
- Craft glue or glue gun

Instructions

1: Center and stitch design, using two strands floss for Cross-Stitch and one strand floss for Backstitch.

Notes: From mounting board, cut one 9¼" x 9¼" piece. From fabric, cut one 1" x 45" bias strip for piping. Line inside of basket with remaining fabric as shown in photo or as desired.

2: Fold bias strip in half lengthwise with wrong sides facing and cord between; sew close to cord, forming piping.

3: Center and mount design over board. Glue piping to back outside edges of mounted design. Position and glue mounted design to front of basket as shown.

Stitch Count:
121 wide x 120 high

Approximate Design Size:
11-count 11" x 11"
14-count 8¾" x 8⅝"·
16-count 7⅝" x 7½"
18-count 6¾" x 6¾"
22-count 5½" x 5½"

X	B'st	DMC®	ANCHOR®	COLORS
■		#310	#403	Black
♥		#312	#979	Very Dk. Baby Blue
▨		#319	#218	Very Dk. Pistachio Green
2		#334	#977	Med. Baby Blue
■		#336	#150	Navy Blue
f		#356	#5975	Med. Terra Cotta
□		#367	#217	Dk. Pistachio Green
▤		#368	#214	Lt. Pistachio Green
▨		#413	#401	Dk. Pewter Gray
3		#414	#235	Dk. Steel Gray
■		#721	#324	Med. Orange Spice
+		#722	#323	Lt. Orange Spice
□		#725	#305	Topaz
h		#739	#387	Ultra Very Lt. Tan
N		#783	#307	Med. Topaz
K		#920	#1004	Med. Copper
★		#3325	#129	Lt. Baby Blue
	◢	#3799	#236	Very Dk. Pewter Gray
O		#3825	#323	Pale Pumpkin
•		White	#2	White

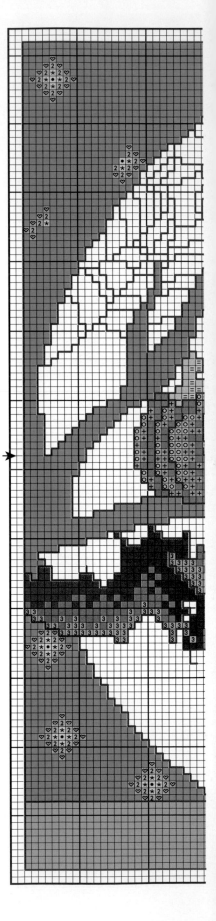

Balloon Fair

DESIGNED BY
MIKE VICKERY

Balloon Fair

Materials
- 12" x 18" piece of light blue 14-count Aida

Instructions
Center and stitch design, using two strands floss for Cross-Stitch and one strand floss for Backstitch.

Stitch Count:
164 wide x 80 high

Approximate Design Size:
11-count 15" x 7⅜"
14-count 11¾" x 5¾"
16-count 10¼" x 5"
18-count 9⅛" x 4½"
22-count 7½" x 3⅝"

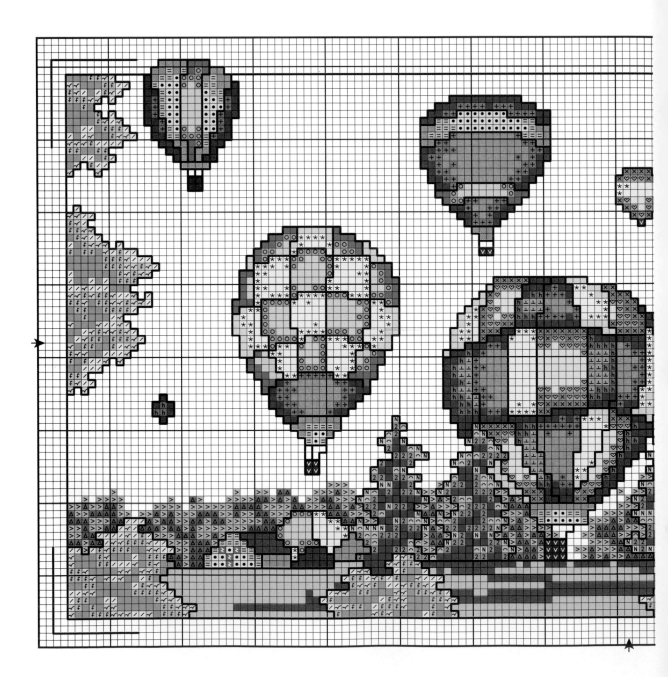

X	DMC®	ANCHOR®	COLORS		X B'st	DMC®	ANCHOR®	COLORS
⊥	#211	#342	Lt. Lavender		▷	#772	#259	Very Lt. Yellow Green
⧈	#310	#403	Black			#783	#307	Med. Topaz
	#319	#218	Very Dk. Pistachio Green		⊙	#813	#161	Lt. Blue
2	#320	#215	Med. Pistachio Green		≡	#822	#390	Lt. Beige Gray
	#349	#13	Dk. Coral			#825	#162	Dk. Blue
+	#351	#10	Coral			#828	#158	Ultra Very Lt. Blue
	#352	#9	Lt. Coral		f	#904	#258	Very Dk. Parrot Green
⌢	#368	#214	Lt. Pistachio Green		f	#905	#257	Dk. Parrot Green
N	#369	#1043	Very Lt. Pistachio Green		✔	#906	#256	Med. Parrot Green
V	#435	#1046	Very Lt. Brown		╱	#907	#255	Lt. Parrot Green
	#470	#267	Lt. Avocado Green		✕	#958	#187	Dk. Sea Green
	#472	#253	Ultra Lt. Avocado Green		♥	#959	#186	Med. Sea Green
	#552	#99	Med. Violet			#964	#185	Lt. Sea Green
h	#554	#96	Lt. Violet		△	#3348	#264	Lt. Yellow Green
	#644	#830	Med. Beige Gray		╱	#3799	#236	Very Dk. Pewter Gray
✶	#725	#305	Topaz		•	White	#2	White
	#727	#293	Very Lt. Topaz					

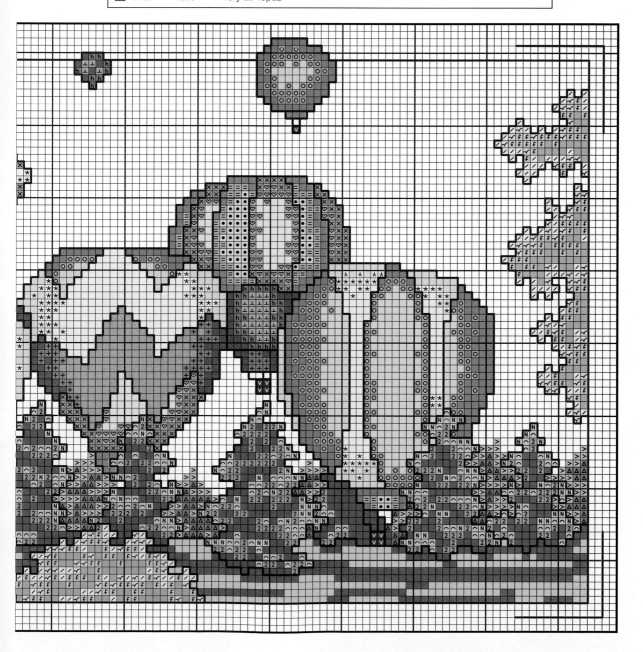

ABC Sampler

DESIGNED BY JUDY GIBBS

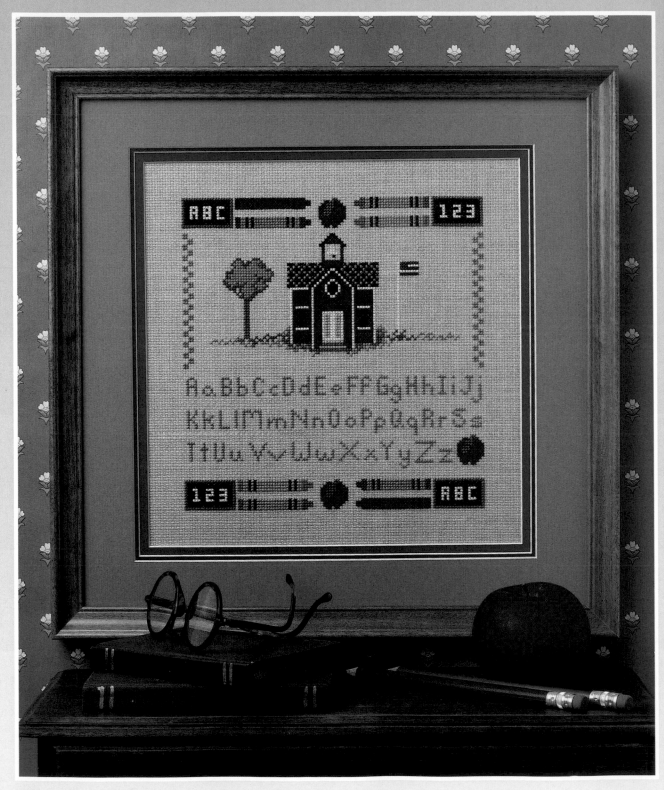

Materials
• 14" x 14" piece of beige 14-count Aida

Instructions
Center and stitch design, using two strands floss for Cross-Stitch and Backstitch.

Stitch Count:
112 wide x 115 high

Approximate Design Size:
11-count 10¼" x 10½"
14-count 8" x 8¼"
16-count 7" x 7¼"
18-count 6¼" x 6⅜"
22-count 5⅛" x 5¼"

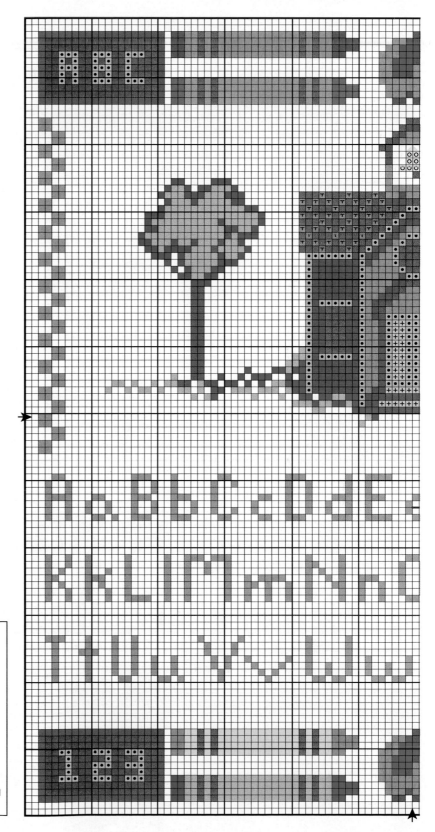

X	B'st	³/₄x	DMC®	ANCHOR®	COLORS
			#310	#403	Black
			#318	#399	Lt. Steel Gray
			#349	#13	Dk. Coral
			#434	#310	Lt. Brown
+			#437	#362	Lt. Tan
			#700	#228	Bright Green
			#703	#238	Chartreuse
O			#726	#295	Lt. Topaz
			#740	#316	Tangerine
			#741	#304	Med. Tangerine
			#798	#131	Dk. Delft Blue
			#809	#130	Delft Blue
			#817	#13	Very Dk. Coral Red
•			White	#2	White

ABC Sampler

X	B'st	3/4x	DMC®	ANCHOR®	COLORS
■			#310	#403	Black
T			#318	#399	Lt. Steel Gray
▨			#349	#13	Dk. Coral
■			#434	#310	Lt. Brown
+			#437	#362	Lt. Tan
▨			#700	#228	Bright Green
▨			#703	#238	Chartreuse
O		□	#726	#295	Lt. Topaz
▨			#740	#316	Tangerine
▨			#741	#304	Med. Tangerine
▨			#798	#131	Dk. Delft Blue
▨	◪		#809	#130	Delft Blue
▨			#817	#13	Very Dk. Coral Red
⊡			White	#2	White

The Needlecraft Shop

CHAPTER
FOUR

Winter
Serenade

Centuries of Santa

DESIGNED BY MIKE VICKERY

Materials
- 15" x 20" piece of tea-dyed 28-count Linen

Instructions
Center and stitch design, stitching over two threads and using two strands floss for Cross-Stitch and one strand floss for Backstitch.

Stitch Count:
189 wide x 121 high

Approximate Design Size:
11-count 17¼" x 11"
14-count 13½" x 8¾"
16-count 11⅞" x 7⅝"
18-count 10½" x 6¾"
22-count 8⅝" x 5½"
28-count over two
   threads 13½" x 8¾"

X	B'st	¼x	DMC®	ANCHOR®	COLORS
h			#310	#403	Black
♥			#312	#979	Very Dk. Baby Blue
S		◪	#319	#218	Very Dk. Pistachio Green
Ø			#320	#215	Med. Pistachio Green
			#334	#977	Med. Baby Blue
T		◪	#336	#150	Navy Blue
◠			#340	#118	Med. Blue Violet
			#341	#117	Lt. Blue Violet
C			#349	#13	Dk. Coral
✚			#351	#10	Coral
			#352	#9	Lt. Coral
╱			#353	#8	Peach
>			#368	#214	Lt. Pistachio Green
△			#413	#401	Dk. Pewter Gray
f			#414	#235	Dk. Steel Gray
W			#415	#398	Pearl Gray
3			#422	#373	Lt. Hazelnut Brown
■		◪	#498	#1005	Dk. Red
⊥			#644	#830	Med. Beige Gray
O			#676	#891	Lt. Old Gold
			#700	#228	Bright Green
✕			#702	#226	Kelly Green
			#704	#256	Bright Chartreuse
✓			#729	#890	Med. Old Gold
⌄			#762	#234	Very Lt. Pearl Gray
			#822	#390	Lt. Beige Gray
Ø			#869	#944	Very Dk. Hazelnut Brown
D			#931	#1034	Med. Antique Blue
T			#932	#1033	Lt. Antique Blue
V			#948	#1011	Very Lt. Peach
■			#3746	#1030	Dk. Blue Violet
K			#3752	#1032	Very Lt. Antique Blue
	╱		#3799	#236	Very Dk. Pewter Gray
		◪	#3820	#306	Dk. Straw
2			#3821	#305	Straw
☆			#3822	#295	Lt. Straw
N			#3828	#888	Hazelnut Brown
●			White	#2	White

Christmas Trims

Designed by Kathleen Hurley

Materials
- 9" x 9" piece of cameo peach 14-count Aida
- 9" x 9" piece of forget-me-not blue 14-count Aida
- 9" x 9" piece of jonquil yellow 14-count Aida
- Three sheets of felt
- Fabric stiffener
- Three 6" pieces of cord
- Craft glue or glue gun

Instructions
1: Center and stitch "Beary Noel" design onto cameo peach Aida; "Snowman" design onto forget-me-not blue Aida; and "Angel Bear" design onto jonquil yellow Aida, using two strands floss for Cross-Stitch and one strand floss for Backstitch and French Knot.

Notes: Trim each design as shown in photo or into desired shape. Trim felt as shown or into desired shape.

2: For each ornament, apply fabric stiffener to trimmed design following manufacturer's instructions. Glue felt to back of each design. For hangers, glue ends of one piece of cord to back of each design.

Beary Noel

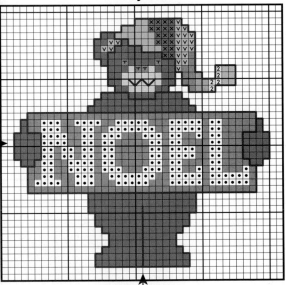

Snowman

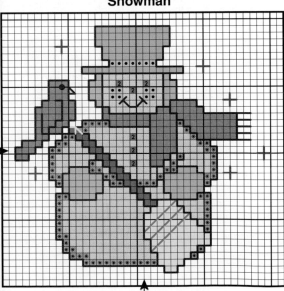

Beary Noel			
X	B'st	DMC®	ANCHOR®	COLORS
T	✓	#310	#403	Black
		#436	#1045	Tan
X		#554	#96	Lt. Violet
		#666	#46	Bright Red
		#704	#256	Bright Chartreuse
		#700	#001	Very Lt. Tan
		#798	#131	Dk. Delft Blue
V		#957	#50	Pale Geranium
		#971	#316	Pumpkin
2		#973	#297	Bright Canary
•		White	#2	White

Angel Bear			
X	B'st	DMC®	ANCHOR®	COLORS
⌣	✓	#310	#403	Black
X		#415	#398	Pearl Gray
		#436	#1045	Tan
		#701	#227	Lt. Green
		#739	#287	Ultra Very Lt. Tan
	✓	#891	#35	Dk. Carnation
O		#893	#28	Lt. Carnation
⊥		#894	#27	Very Lt. Carnation
•		#5284		Gold Dk. Metallic
		White	#2	White

Snowman				
X	B'st	1/4x	Fr	DMC®	ANCHOR®	COLORS
2	✓		●	#310	#403	Black
✳		⁄		#415	#398	Pearl Gray
				#436	#1045	Tan
	✓			#666	#46	Bright Red
				#701	#227	Lt. Green
	✓			#798	#131	Dk. Delft Blue
•				#957	#50	Pale Geranium
	⁄	⁄		#972	#298	Deep Canary
	⁄			#5283	#702	Silver Metallic
				White	#2	White

Beary Noel & Snowman Stitch Count:
38 wide x 37 high

Approximate Design Size:
11-count 3½" x 3⅜"
14-count 2¾" x 2¾"
16-count 2⅜" x 2⅜"
18-count 2⅛" x 2⅛"
22-count 1¾" x 1¾"

Angel Bear Stitch Count:
38 wide x 42 high

Approximate Design Size:
11-count 3½" x 3⅞"
14-count 2¾" x 3"
16-count 2⅜" x 2⅝"
18-count 2⅛" x 2⅜"
22-count 1¾" x 2"

Angel Bear

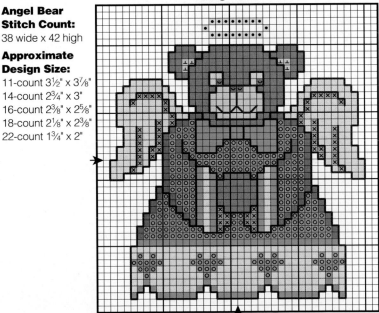

Dutch Memories

DESIGNED BY KATHLEEN HURLEY

Materials for One

- 11" x 13" piece of white 28-count Lugana®
- Mounting board
- Batting
- ¾ yd. decorative trim
- 8" x 10" fabric-covered photo album
- Craft glue or glue gun

Instructions

1: Center and stitch design of choice, stitching over two threads and using two strands floss for Cross-Stitch and one strand floss for Backstitch and French Knot.

Note: From mounting board and batting, cut one each following oval shape of design as shown in photo.

2: Center and mount design over batting and board. Glue decorative trim to outside edge of mounted design. Position and glue mounted design to photo album as shown.

Hein & Matje Stitch Count:
72 wide x 97 high

Approximate Design Size:
11-count 6⅝" x 8⅞"
14-count 5¼" x 7"
16-count 4½" x 6⅛"
18-count 4" x 5⅜"
22-count 3⅜" x 4½"
28-count over two threads 5¼" x 7"

X	B'st	¼x	Fr	DMC®	ANCHOR®	COLORS		X	B'st	¼x	DMC®	ANCHOR®	COLORS
2	✓		●	#310	#403	Black				✓	#817	#13	Very Dk. Coral Red
		◤		#351	#10	Coral			✓		#902	#897	Very Dk. Garnet
		◤		#415	#398	Pearl Gray		✓	✓	◤	#938	#381	Ultra Dk. Coffee Brown
		◤		#435	#1046	Very Lt. Brown		●			#957	#50	Pale Geranium
T		◤		#437	#362	Lt. Tan			✓		#3345	#268	Dk. Hunter Green
				#726	#295	Lt. Topaz		O			#3347	#266	Med. Yellow Green
				#727	#293	Very Lt. Topaz				◤	#3348	#264	Lt. Yellow Green
				#754	#1012	Lt. Peach		✕			#3776	#1048	Lt. Mahogany
		◤		#798	#131	Dk. Delft Blue				◤	White	#2	White
				#809	#130	Delft Blue							

Hein

X	B'st	1/4x	Fr	DMC®	ANCHOR®	COLORS	X	B'st	1/4x	DMC®	ANCHOR®	COLORS
2	✓		●	#310	#403	Black			✓	#817	#13	Very Dk. Coral Red
		✓		#351	#10	Coral			✓	#902	#897	Very Dk. Garnet
		✓		#415	#398	Pearl Gray	✓		✓	#938	#381	Ultra Dk. Coffee Brown
		✓		#435	#1046	Very Lt. Brown	●			#957	#50	Pale Geranium
T		✓		#437	#362	Lt. Tan			✓	#3345	#268	Dk. Hunter Green
		✓		#726	#295	Lt. Topaz	O			#3347	#266	Med. Yellow Green
		✓		#727	#293	Very Lt. Topaz				#3348	#264	Lt. Yellow Green
		✓		#754	#1012	Lt. Peach	X			#3776	#1048	Lt. Mahogany
		✓		#798	#131	Dk. Delft Blue			✓	White	#2	White
		✓		#809	#130	Delft Blue						

Matje

Merry Santa

Designed by Tom & Felicia Williams

Merry Santa

Materials
- 14" x 17" piece of white 14-count Aida
- ½ yd. fabric
- ½ yd. lining fabric
- 1¼ yds. decorative trim
- Batting

Instructions

1: Center and stitch design, using two strands floss or one strand Wisper for Cross-Stitch. Use one strand floss for Backstitch. Use one strand coordinating floss for securing beads.

Notes: Trim design 1½" from outside edges following shape of design as shown in photo for front. From fabric, cut one same as front for back. From lining fabric and batting,

X	¼x	DMC®	ANCHOR®	COLORS
		#208	#110	Very Dk. Lavender
		#210	#108	Med. Lavender
		#307	#289	Lemon
		#310	#403	Black
		#321	#9046	Red
		#444	#290	Dk. Lemon
		#498	#1005	Dk. Red
		#754	#1012	Lt. Peach
		#799	#136	Med. Delft Blue
		#800	#144	Pale Delft Blue
		#829	#906	Very Dk. Golden Olive
		#832	#888	Golden Olive
		#890	#218	Ultra Dk. Pistachio Green
		#909	#923	Very Dk. Emerald Green

X	B'st	¼x	DMC®	ANCHOR®	RAINBOW GALLERY	COLORS
			#911	#205		Med. Emerald Green
			#913	#204		Med. Nile Green
			#946	#332		Med. Burnt Orange
			#951	#1010		Lt. Tawny
			#970	#316		Lt. Pumpkin
			#3371	#382		Black Brown
			#3801	#35		Very Dk. Melon
			#5282	#701		Gold Metallic
					#W88(Wisper)	White

MILL HILL SEED BEADS

#00081	Jet
#02012	Royal Plum

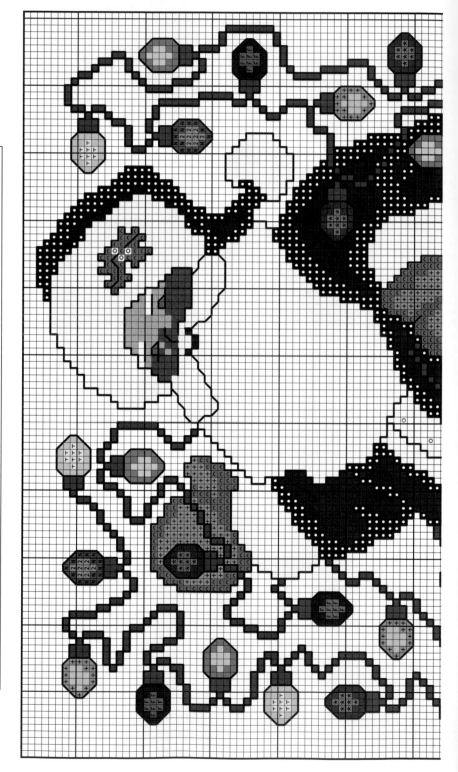

cut two each same as front.
Use ½" seam allowance.

2: Baste batting and lining to
wrong side of front and back.
With right sides facing, sew
decorative trim around top and
side edges of front. With right
sides facing, sew front and back
together, leaving bottom edge
open; turn right sides out. Press
under ½" hem on bottom edge;
sew in place. Sew trim to bot
tom edge of front.

Stitch Count:
107 wide x 154 high

**Approximate
Design Size:**
11-count 9¾" x 14"
14-count 7¾" x 11"
16-count 6¾" x 9⅝"
18-count 6" x 8⅝"
22-count 4⅞" x 7"

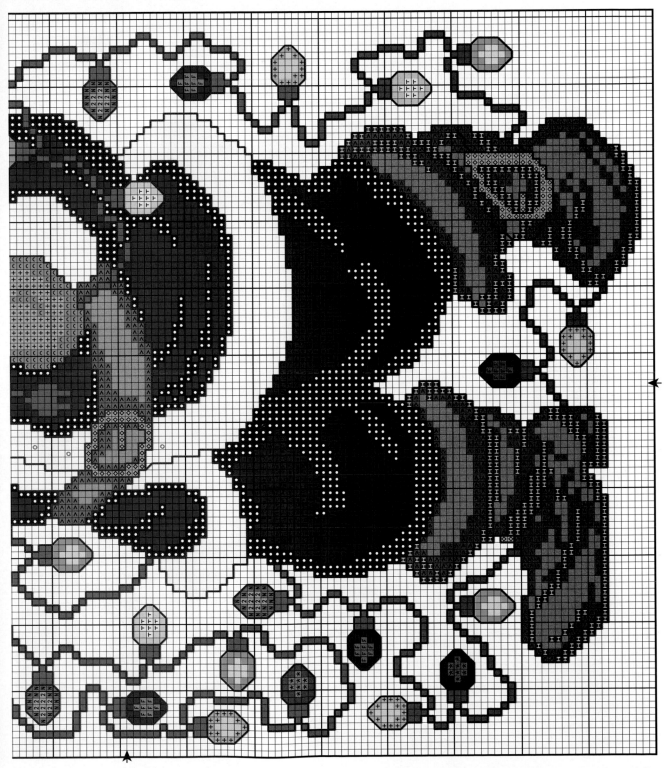

Be Mine

Designed by Tom & Felicia Williams

Materials
- 11" x 13" piece of white 14-count Aida
- Jumper pattern (Butterick® No. 6106 was used)

Instructions

1: Center and stitch design, using two strands floss for Cross-Stitch and one strand floss for Back-stitch and French Knot.

Notes: Follow Butterick No. 6106 pattern view "I" for materials and construction. Trim design to 6⅛" x 8½".

2: Center and piece design with fabric; trim following Jumper Bib No. 1 pattern piece. Construct jumper following pattern instructions.

Stitch Count:
65 wide x 99 high

Approximate Design Size:
11-count 6" x 9"
14-count 4¾" x 7⅛"
16-count 4⅛" x 6¼"
18-count 3⅝" x 5½"
22-count 3" x 4½"

X	B'st	¼x	Fr	DMC®	ANCHOR®	COLORS
●		◣		#310	#403	Black
	◢			#347	#1025	Very Dk. Salmon
V				#353	#8	Peach
⌂				#677	#886	Very Lt. Old Gold
				#746	#275	Off White
		◣		#761	#1021	Lt. Salmon
Y				#813	#161	Lt. Blue
				#828	#158	Ultra Very Lt. Blue
		◣		#948	#1011	Very Lt. Peach
	◢		●	#3371	#382	Black Brown
O				#3712	#1023	Med. Salmon
				#3820	#306	Dk. Straw
⊥				#3822	#295	Lt. Straw

Winter Skating

DESIGNED BY MIKE VICKERY

Winter Skating

Materials

- One 9" x 14" piece and one 13" x 16" piece of white 27-count Meran
- Mirror with 12" x 9" design opening
- Wooden box with 3" x 7¾" design opening

Instructions

Note: For Box, choose motif design of choice from graph and chart onto graph paper for proper placement.

1: Center and stitch design onto 13" x 16" piece for

Stitch Count:
135 wide x 95 high

Approximate Design Size:
11-count 12⅜" x 8⅝"
14-count 9¾" x 6⅞"
16-count 8½" x 6"
18-count 7½" x 5⅜"
22-count 6⅛" x 4⅜"
27-count over two
 threads 10" x 7⅛"

X	B'st	DMC®	ANCHOR®	COLORS
■		#310	#403	Black
■		#334	#977	Med. Baby Blue
■		#349	#13	Dk. Coral
■		#351	#10	Coral
W		#353	#8	Peach
▨		#356	#5975	Med. Terra Cotta
▨		#368	#214	Lt. Pistachio Green
⧖		#414	#235	Dk. Steel Gray
∥		#553	#98	Violet
▨		#554	#96	Lt. Violet
✳		#644	#830	Med. Beige Gray
K		#645	#273	Very Dk. Beaver Gray
∨		#647	#1040	Med. Beaver Gray
✕		#700	#228	Bright Green
△		#702	#226	Kelly Green
2		#725	#305	Topaz
◇		#727	#293	Very Lt. Topaz
F		#758	#882	Very Lt. Terra Cotta
☐		#775	#128	Very Lt. Baby Blue
♥		#776	#24	Med. Pink
+		#818	#23	Baby Pink
☐		#822	#390	Lt. Beige Gray
■		#926	#850	Med. Gray Green
◨		#928	#274	Very Lt. Gray Green
D		#948	#1011	Very Lt. Peach
▷		#958	#187	Dk. Seagreen
H		#964	#185	Lt. Seagreen
■		#986	#246	Very Dk. Forest Green
○		#988	#243	Med. Forest Green
☆		#3072	#847	Very Lt. Beaver Gray
●		#3325	#129	Lt. Baby Blue
T		#3347	#266	Med. Yellow Green
✓		#3348	#264	Lt. Yellow Green
■		#3787	#393	Dk. Brown Gray
	✎	#3799	#236	Very Dk. Pewter Gray
☐		White	#2	White

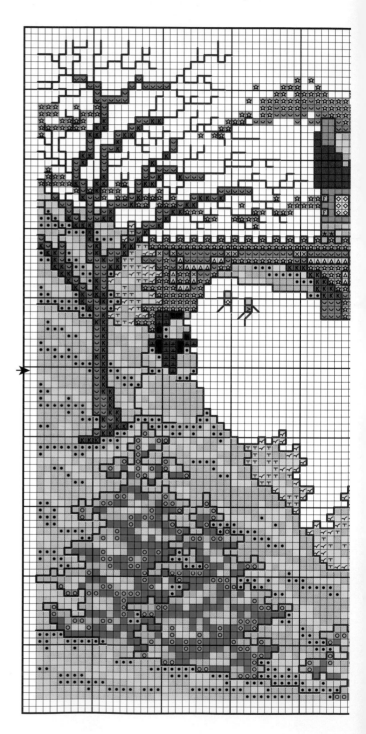

Mirror; and design of choice onto 9" x 14" piece of Meran for Box, stitching over two threads and using two strands floss for Cross-Stitch and one strand floss for Backstitch.

2: For Mirror, position and secure design in mirror following manufacturer's instructions.

ing manufacturer's instructions.

3: For Box, position and secure design in box following manufacturer's instructions.

Hot Cocoa

Designed by Christine A. Hendricks

Materials
- 11" x 14" piece of beige 14-count Aida
- Apron pattern (Simplicity® Crafts pattern No. 7889 was used)

Instructions
1: Center and stitch design, using two strands floss or two strands blending filament for Cross-Stitch and one strand floss for Backstitch and French Knot.

Notes: Follow Simplicity Crafts No. 7889 pattern view "E" for materials and construction. Trim design to 6¾" x 9¾".

2: Center and piece design with fabric; trim following Apron Bib Front No. 12 pattern piece. Construct apron following pattern instructions.

Quick Cocoa Mix

1 lb. chocolate milk/cocoa mix
8 oz. powdered creamer
1½ c. powdered sugar
1 (8 qt.) box dry milk

Mix dry ingredients together. Pour into decorative containers and give as gifts to family, friends and neighbors. Attach a note instructing to add desired amount of mixture to a cup of hot water.

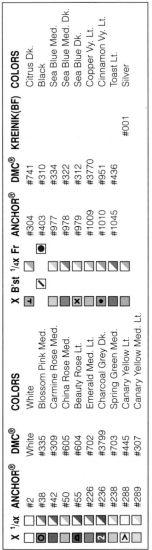

Stitch Count:
109 wide x 65 high

Approximate Design Size:
11-count 10" x 6"
14-count 7⅞" x 4¾"
16-count 6⅞" x 4⅛"
18-count 6⅛" x 3⅝"
22-count 5" x 3"

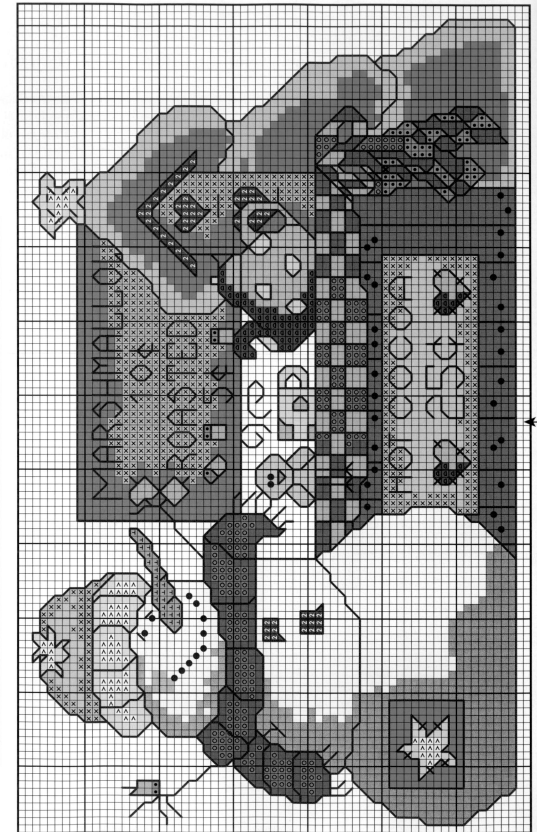

Country Kitchen

DESIGNED BY TOM & FELICIA WILLIAMS

Country Kitchen

Materials
- One 6" x 9" piece, one 14" x 17" piece and one 18" x 18" piece of country oatmeal 14-count Royal Classic
- Snap-together acrylic napkin ring with white 14-count Vinyl-Weave™ insert
- Place mat and napkin

Instructions
Note: For Place Mat, Bread Cloth and Napkin Ring, choose motif designs of choice from graph and chart onto graph paper for proper placement.

1: Center and stitch design onto 14" x 17" piece for Sampler; design of choice onto 6" x 9" piece for Place Mat; design of choice onto 18" x 18" piece of Royal Classic for Bread Cloth; and design of choice

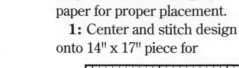

Stitch Count:
115 wide x 147 high

Approximate Design Size:
11-count 10½" x 13⅜"
14-count 8¼" x 10½"
16-count 7¼" x 9¼"
18-count 6⅜" x 8¼"
22-count 5¼" x 6¾"

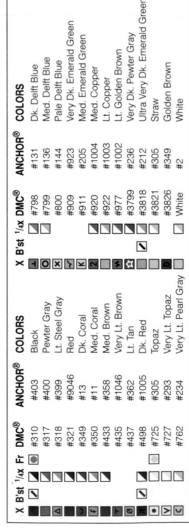

X	B'st	¼x	Fr	DMC®	ANCHOR®	COLORS
			●	#310	#403	Black
				#317	#400	Pewter Gray
				#318	#399	Lt. Steel Gray
				#321	#9046	Red
				#349	#13	Dk. Coral
				#350	#11	Med. Coral
				#433	#358	Med. Brown
				#435	#1046	Very Lt. Brown
				#437	#362	Lt. Tan
				#498	#1005	Dk. Red
			□	#725	#305	Topaz
				#727	#293	Very Lt. Topaz
				#762	#234	Very Lt. Pearl Gray

X	B'st	¼x	DMC®	ANCHOR®	COLORS
			#798	#131	Dk. Delft Blue
			#799	#136	Med. Delft Blue
			#800	#144	Pale Delft Blue
			#909	#923	Very Dk. Emerald Green
			#911	#205	Med. Emerald Green
			#920	#1004	Med. Copper
			#922	#1003	Lt. Copper
			#977	#1002	Lt. Golden Brown
			#3799	#236	Very Dk. Pewter Gray
			#3818	#212	Ultra Very Dk. Emerald Green
			#3821	#305	Straw
			#3826	#349	Golden Brown
			White	#2	White

onto vinyl weave insert for Napkin Ring, using two strands floss for Cross-Stitch and one strand floss for Backstitch and French Knot.

2: For Place Mat, press under ½" on design edges; position and sew to front of place mat as shown in photo.

3: For Bread Cloth, stay stitch ½" from edges; fray edges.

4: For Napkin Ring, assemble napkin ring following manufacturer's instructions.

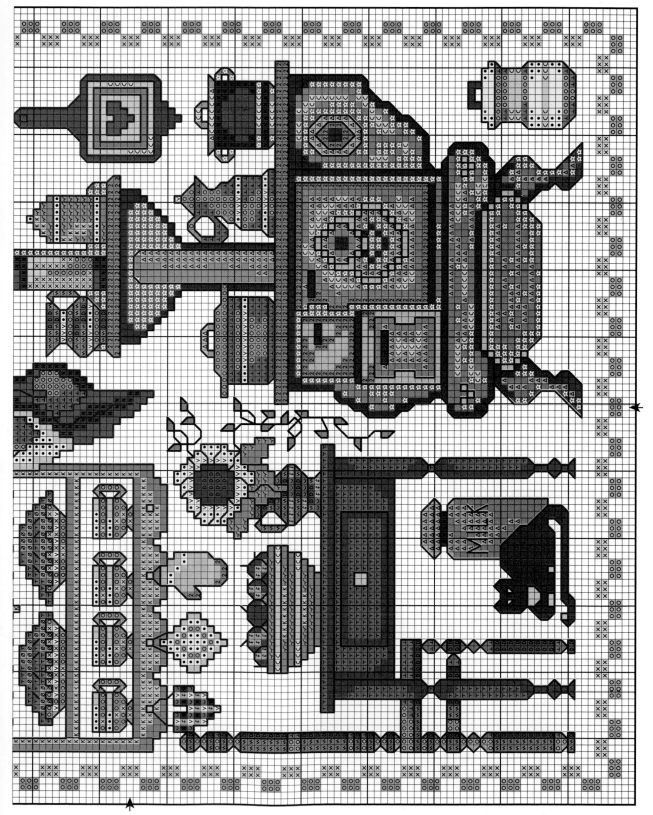

Seasons

Designed by Mike Vickery

Materials
• 15" x 15" piece of antique white 28-count Jobelan®

Instructions
Center and stitch design, stitching over two threads and using two strands floss for Cross-Stitch and one strand floss for Backstitch.

Stitch Count:
118 wide x 118 high

Approximate Design Size:
11-count 10¾" x 10¾"
14-count 8½" x 8½"
16-count 7⅜" x 7⅜"
18-count 6⅝" x 6⅝"
22-count 5⅜" x 5⅜"
28-count over two
  threads 8½" x 8½"

X	B'st	¼x	DMC®	ANCHOR®	COLORS
⊥		◪	#307	#289	Lemon
◖			#310	#403	Black
▨			#334	#977	Med. Baby Blue
▨			#367	#217	Dk. Pistachio Green
△			#368	#214	Lt. Pistachio Green
●		◪	#445	#288	Lt. Lemon
■		◪	#498	#1005	Dk. Red
2		◪	#581	#280	Moss Green
+		◪	#666	#46	Bright Red
▨			#700	#228	Bright Green
▧			#702	#226	Kelly Green
▨			#704	#256	Bright Chartreuse
f		◪	#725	#305	Topaz
▢		◻	#727	#293	Very Lt. Topaz
☆		◪	#741	#304	Med. Tangerine
⌣		◪	#742	#303	Lt. Tangerine
�			#743	#302	Med. Yellow
K		◻	#772	#259	Very Lt. Yellow Green
▨			#775	#128	Very Lt. Baby Blue
▨			#783	#307	Med. Topaz
▨			#910	#229	Dk. Emerald Green
×			#912	#209	Lt. Emerald Green
▢			#954	#203	Nile Green
○			#3325	#129	Lt. Baby Blue
▨		◪	#3705	#35	Dk. Melon
	◪		#3799	#236	Very Dk. Pewter Gray
◭		◪	#3819	#279	Lt. Moss Green
V		◻	White	#2	White

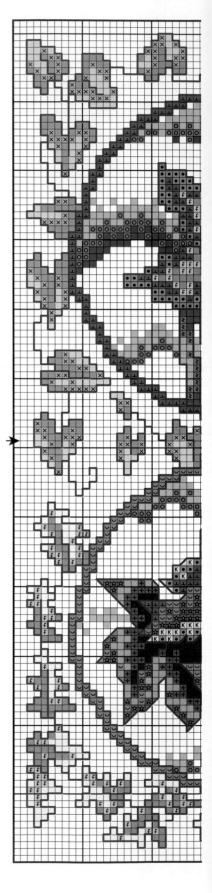

Roses are Red...

DESIGNED BY KATHLEEN HURLEY

Materials

- 13" x 15" piece of antique white 28-count Quaker Cloth
- 1½ yds. fabric
- 1¾ yds. lace
- 12" x 12" pillow form

Instructions

1: Center and stitch design, stitching over two threads and using two strands floss for Cross-Stitch and Backstitch and French Knot of lettering. Use one strand floss for remaining Backstitch and Straight Stitch.

Notes: Trim design to 8½" x 10½". From fabric, cut two 2½" x 13½" for A pieces, two 3½" x 10½" for B pieces, two 9½" x 13½" pieces for back and one 7" x 135" piece for ruffle (piecing is necessary). Use ½" seam allowance.

2: With right sides facing, sew design, A and B pieces together according to Front Assembly Diagram, forming front.

3: For ruffle, with right sides facing, sew short ends of fabric piece together, forming ring. Fold wrong sides together; press. Gather unfinished edges to fit around outside edges of front.

4: With right sides facing, sew to front, first lace then ruffle.

5: Hem one 13½" edge of each back piece. Place one hemmed edge over the other, overlapping enough to create a 13½" x 13½" back with opening. Baste outside edges together; press.

6: With right sides facing, sew front and back together. Trim seam and turn right sides out; press. Insert pillow form.

Stitch Count:
95 wide x 121 high

Approximate Design Size:
11-count 8⅝" x 11"
14-count 6⅞" x 8¾"
16-count 6" x 7⅝"
18-count 5⅜" x 6¾"
22-count 4⅜" x 5½"
28-count over two threads 6⅞" x 8¾"

Front Assembly Diagram

X	B'st	1/4x	Str	Fr	DMC®	ANCHOR®	COLORS
■		◩			#309	#42	Dk. Rose
S	✓	◩	✓	●	#310	#403	Black
		◩			#320	#215	Med. Pistachio Green
☆		◩			#368	#214	Lt. Pistachio Green
★	✓	◩			#415	#398	Pearl Gray
Ø	✓	◩			#434	#310	Lt. Brown
		◩			#550	#102	Very Dk. Violet
↰		◩			#553	#98	Violet
K		◩			#554	#96	Lt. Violet
C		◩			#726	#295	Lt. Topaz
F		☐			#727	#293	Very Lt. Topaz
+		◩			#740	#316	Tangerine
V		◩			#742	#303	Lt. Tangerine
•		◩			#754	#1012	Lt. Peach
D		◩			#760	#1022	Salmon
h		◩			#776	#24	Med. Pink
	✓				#796	#133	Dk. Royal Blue
>		◩			#797	#132	Royal Blue
■		◩			#799	#136	Med. Delft Blue
		◩			#800	#144	Pale Delft Blue
T		◩			#899	#52	Med. Rose
▲		◩			#948	#1011	Very Lt. Peach
♥		◩			#3328	#1024	Dk. Salmon
	✓				#3345	#268	Dk. Hunter Green
O		◩			#3347	#266	Med. Yellow Green
		◩			#3348	#264	Lt. Yellow Green
±		◩			#3607	#87	Lt. Plum
2		◩			#3609	#85	Ultra Lt. Plum
	✓				#3685	#1028	Very Dk. Mauve
∧		☐			#3865	#2	Winter White

Merry Christmas Stocking

DESIGNED BY KATHLEEN HURLEY

Merry Christmas Stocking

Materials
- 12" x 14" piece of white 11-count Aida
- ½ yd. fabric
- ½ yd. lining fabric
- 1½ yds. piping

Instructions

1: Center and stitch design, using four strands floss for Cross-Stitch and two strands floss for Backstitch and French Knot.

Notes: Trim design into a stocking shape as shown in photo for front. From fabric, cut one same as front for back. From lining fabric, cut two same as front for lining front and back. Use ½" seam allowance.

2: With right sides facing, sew piping to side and bottom edges of front.

3: With right sides facing, sew front and back together, leaving top open, forming stocking; turn right sides out. Repeat with lining front and back pieces, forming lining.

4: With right sides facing, sew piping to top edge of stocking.

5: With right sides facing, sew stocking and lining together around top edge, leaving an opening for turning. Turn right sides out; slip stitch opening closed. Hang as desired.

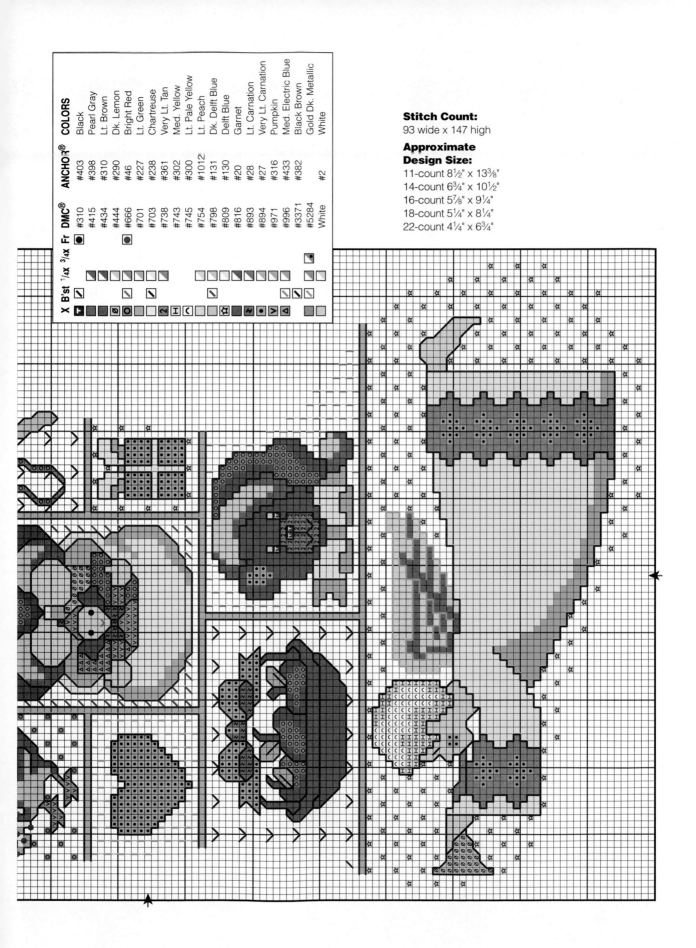

X	B'st	¹/4x	³/4x	Fr	DMC®	ANCHOR®	COLORS
				●	#310	#403	Black
					#415	#398	Pearl Gray
				●	#434	#310	Lt. Brown
					#444	#290	Dk. Lemon
					#666	#46	Bright Red
					#701	#227	Lt. Green
					#703	#238	Chartreuse
					#738	#361	Very Lt. Tan
					#743	#302	Med. Yellow
					#745	#300	Lt. Pale Yellow
					#754	#1012	Lt. Peach
					#798	#131	Dk. Delft Blue
					#809	#130	Delft Blue
					#816	#20	Garnet
					#893	#28	Lt. Carnation
					#894	#27	Very Lt. Carnation
					#971	#316	Pumpkin
					#996	#433	Med. Electric Blue
					#3371	#382	Black Brown
					#5284	#2	Gold Dk. Metallic
					White		White

Stitch Count:
93 wide x 147 high

Approximate Design Size:
11-count 8½" x 13⅜"
14-count 6¾" x 10½"
16-count 5⅞" x 9¼"
18-count 5¼" x 8¼"
22-count 4¼" x 6¾"

Holiday Reflections

DESIGNED BY KATHLEEN HURLEY

Materials

- 11" x 13" piece of gold/cream 20-count Valerie
- Wooden candle screen with 5" x 7" design opening

Instructions

Center and stitch design, stitching over two threads and using two strands floss for Cross-Stitch, Backstitch of ornament hangers and candlewicks and Straight Stitch. Use one strand floss for remaining Backstitch. Position and secure design in candle screen following manufacturer's instructions.

Stitch Count:
50 wide x 70 high

Approximate Design Size:
11-count 4⅝" x 6⅜"
14-count 3⅝" x 5"
16-count 3⅛" x 4⅜"
18-count 2⅞" x 4"
22-count 2⅜" x 3¼"
20-count over two threads 5" x 7"

X	B'st	Str	DMC®	ANCHOR®	COLORS
■	✓		#304	#1006	Med. Red
▨	✓		#334	#977	Med. Baby Blue
▨	✓		#666	#46	Bright Red
△	✓		#899	#52	Med. Rose
▨		✓	#909	#923	Very Dk. Emerald Green
●	✓		#912	#209	Lt. Emerald Green
□	✓		#972	#298	Deep Canary
○	✓		#973	#297	Bright Canary
▷	✓		#5282	#701	Gold Metallic
+			White	#2	White

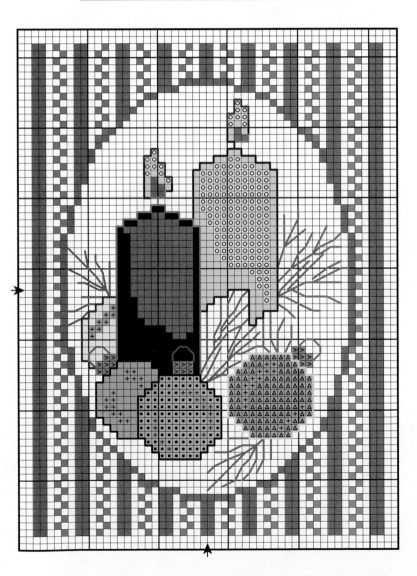

Poinsettia

Designed by Mike Vickery

Home Sampler

DESIGNED BY LOIS WINSTON

Materials

- 11" x 12" piece of white 14-count Aida

Instructions

Center and stitch design, using two strands floss for Cross-Stitch and one strand floss for Backstitch.

X	B'st	ANCHOR®	DMC®	COLORS
>		#262	#3052	Loden Green Med.
■		#358	#433	Coffee
	✓	#403	#310	Black
T		#871	#3041	Amethyst Med. Lt.
■		#872	#3740	Amethyst Med.
■		#879	#500	Pine Dk.
O		#895	#223	Rose Wine Med.
■		#896	#3721	Rose Wine Dk.
■		#921	#931	Denim Med.

Stitch Count:
69 wide x 89 high

Approximate Design Size:
11-count 6⅜" x 8⅛"
14-count 5" x 6⅜"
16-count 4⅜" x 5⅝"
18-count 3⅞" x 5"
22-count 3⅛" x 4⅛"

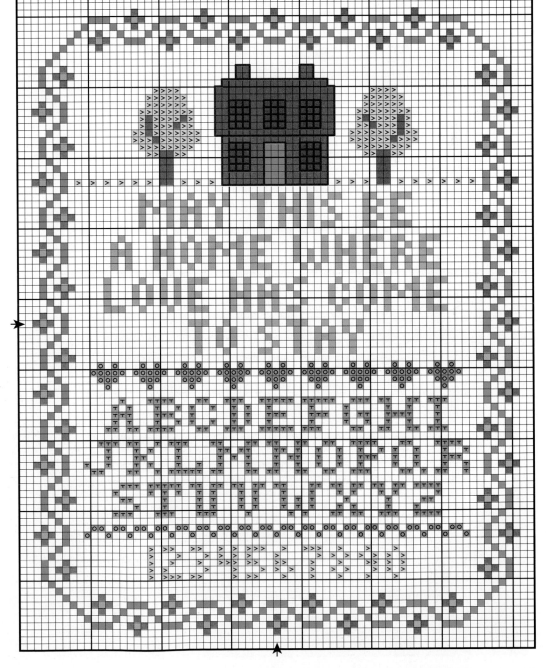

Pansy Keepsakes

DESIGNED BY CAROLE RODGERS

Materials

- 9" x 9" piece of white 14-count Aida
- 7" x 7" piece of white 22-count Hardanger
- Glass jar with 2⅝" design opening
- Brooch with ⅞" x 1¼" design opening

Instructions

1: Center and stitch "Jar" design onto Aida, using two strands floss for Cross-Stitch and one strand floss for Backstitch, Straight Stitch and Modified Eyelet Stitch. Position and secure design in jar following manufacturer's instructions.

2: Center and stitch "Brooch" design onto Hardanger, using one strand floss for Cross-Stitch, Backstitch and Straight Stitch. Position and secure design in brooch following manufacturer's instructions.

Jar

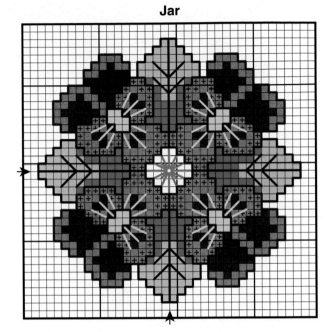

Jar
Stitch Count:
34 wide x 34 high

Approximate Design Size:
11-count 3⅛" x 3⅛"
14-count 2½" x 2½"
16-count 2⅛" x 2⅛"
18-count 2" x 2"
22-count 1⅝" x 1⅝"

X	B'st	Str	Eye	DMC®	ANCHOR®	COLORS
■	✎			#550	#102	Very Dk. Violet
■				#552	#99	Med. Violet
+				#554	#96	Lt. Violet
■		✎		#725	#305	Topaz
■	✎		✎	#986	#246	Very Dk. Forest Green
■				#988	#243	Med. Forest Green

Brooch
Stitch Count:
16 wide x 16 high

Approximate Design Size:
11-count 1½" x 1½"
14-count 1¼" x 1¼"
16-count 1" x 1"
18-count 1" x 1"
22-count ¾" x ¾"

Brooch

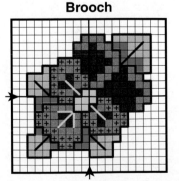

Beaded Ensemble

Designed by Carole Rodgers

Materials

- One 9" x 9" piece and one 12" x 12" piece of red 28-count Evenweave fabric
- Crystal jar with 2⅝" design opening

Instructions

1: Center and stitch "Basket Cloth" design onto one corner of 12" x 12" piece beginning 1¼" from edges; and "Jar" design onto 9" x 9" piece of Evenweave fabric, using one strand fine braid for Cross-Stitch. Use one strand coordinating floss for securing beads.

2: For Basket Cloth, stay stitch ⅝" from edges; fray edges.

3: For Jar, position and secure design in jar following manufacturer's instructions.

Jar

Jar
Stitch Count:
35 wide x 35 high

Approximate Design Size:
11-count 3¼" x 3¼"
14-count 2½" x 2½"
16-count 2¼" x 2¼"
18-count 2" x 2"
22-count 1⅝" x 1⅝"
28-count over two threads 2½" x 2½"

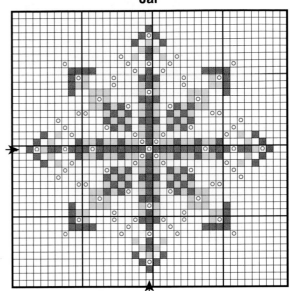

Basket Cloth
Stitch Count:
49 wide x 49 high

Approximate Design Size:
11-count 4½" x 4½"
14-count 3½" x 3½"
16-count 3⅛" x 3⅛"
18-count 2¾" x 2¾"
22-count 2¼" x 2¼"
28-count over two threads 3½" x 3½"

X	½x	KREINIK(#8)	COLORS
■	◿	#001	Silver
▨		#002	Gold

MILL HILL SEED BEADS

◎	#00479	White

Basket Cloth

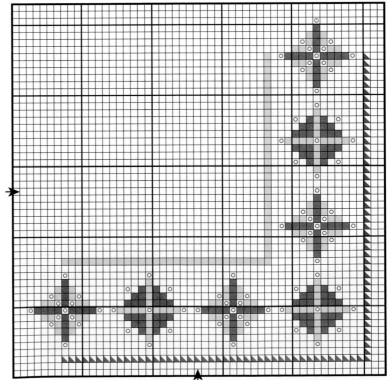

Wolves

DESIGNED BY
MIKE VICKERY

Materials

- 15" x 16" piece of white 11-count Aida

Instructions

Center and stitch design, using four strands floss for Cross-Stitch and two strands floss for Backstitch.

Stitch Count:
110 wide x 95 high

Approximate Design Size:
11-count 10" x 8⅝"
14-count 7⅞" x 6⅞"
16-count 6⅞" x 6"
18-count 6⅛" x 5⅜"
22-count 5" x 4⅜"

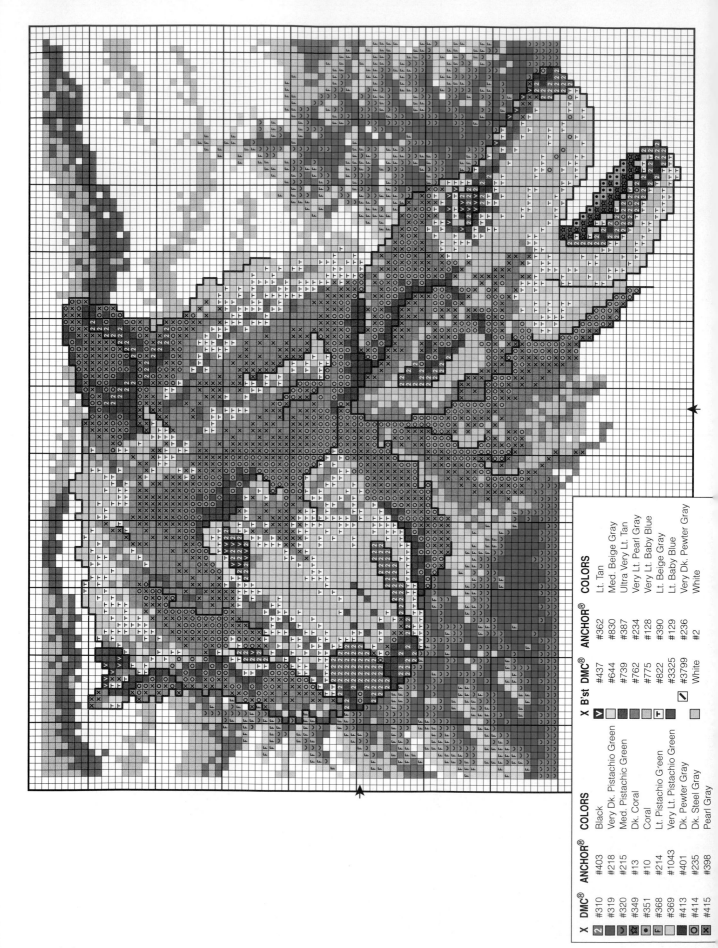

X	DMC®	ANCHOR®	COLORS
2	#310	#403	Black
	#319	#218	Very Dk. Pistachio Green
	#320	#215	Med. Pistachio Green
	#349	#13	Dk. Coral
	#351	#10	Coral
	#368	#214	Lt. Pistachio Green
	#369	#1043	Very Lt. Pistachio Green
	#413	#401	Dk. Pewter Gray
	#414	#235	Dk. Steel Gray
	#415	#398	Pearl Gray

X	B'st	DMC®	ANCHOR®	COLORS
		#437	#362	Lt. Tan
		#644	#830	Med. Beige Gray
		#739	#387	Ultra Very Lt. Tan
		#762	#234	Very Lt. Pearl Gray
		#775	#128	Very Lt. Baby Blue
		#822	#390	Lt. Beige Gray
		#3325	#129	Lt. Baby Blue
		#3799	#236	Very Dk. Pewter Gray
		White	#2	White

General Instructions

Tools of the Stitcher

Fabrics

Most counted cross-stitch projects are worked on evenweave fabrics made especially for counted thread embroidery. These fabrics have vertical and horizontal threads of uniform thickness and spacing. Aida cloth is a favorite of beginning stitchers because its weave forms distinctive squares in the fabric, which makes placing stitches easy. To determine a fabric's thread count, count the number of threads per inch of fabric.

Linen is made from fibers of the flax plant and is strong and durable. Its lasting quality makes it the perfect choice for heirloom projects. Linen is available in a range of muted colors and stitch counts.

In addition to evenweave fabrics, many stitchers enjoy using waste canvas and perforated paper. Waste canvas is basted to clothing or other fabric, forming a grid for stitching which is later removed. Perforated paper has holes evenly spaced for 14 stitches per inch.

Needles

Cross-stitch needles should have elongated eyes and blunt points. They should slip easily between the threads of the fabric, but should not pierce the fabric. The most common sizes used for cross-stitching are size 24 or 26. The ideal needle size is just small enough to slip easily through your fabric. Some stitchers prefer to use a slightly smaller needle for backstitching. When stitching on waste canvas, use a sharp needle.

Hoops, Frames & Scissors

Hoops can be round or oval and come in many sizes. The three main types are plastic, spring-tension and wooden. Frames are easier on the fabric than hoops and come in many sizes and shapes. Once fabric is mounted it doesn't have to be removed until stitching is complete, saving fabric from excessive handling.

Small, sharp scissors are essential for cutting floss and removing mistakes. For cutting fabrics, invest in a top-quality pair of medium-sized sewing scissors. To keep them in top form, use these scissors only for cutting fabrics and floss.

Stitching Threads

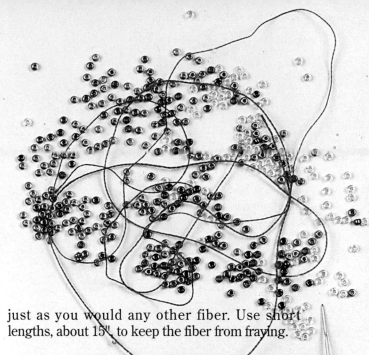

Today's cross-stitcher can achieve a vast array of effects in texture, color and shine. In addition to the perennial favorite, six-strand floss, stitchers can choose from sparkling metallics, shiny rayons, silks, narrow ribbon threads and much more.

Six-Strand Floss

Six-strand floss comes in a variety of colors and is available in metallics, silk and rayon as well as cotton. Most projects are worked using two or three strands of floss for cross-stitches and one or two strands for backstitches. For ease of stitching and to prevent wear on fibers, use lengths no longer than 18".

Pearl Cotton

Pearl cotton is available in #3, #5, #8 and #12, with #3 being the thickest. The plies of pearl cotton will not separate, and for most stitching one strand is used. Pearl cotton has a lustrous sheen.

Flower & Ribbon Threads

Flower thread has a tight twist and comes in many soft colors. It is heavier than one ply of six-strand floss – one strand of flower thread equals two strands of floss. Ribbon thread is a narrow ribbon especially created for stitching. It comes in a large number of colors in satin as well as metallic finishes.

Blending Filament & Metallic Braid

Blending filament is a fine, shiny fiber that can be used alone or combined with floss or other thread. Knotting the blending filament on the needle with a slipknot is recommended for control.

Metallic braid is a braided metallic fiber, usually used single-ply. Thread this fiber

SLIPKNOT

just as you would any other fiber. Use short lengths, about 15", to keep the fiber from fraying.

Stitching with Beads

Small seed beads can be added to any cross-stitch design, using one bead per stitch. Knot thread at beginning of beaded section for security, especially if you are adding beads to clothing. The bead should lie in the same direction as the top half of cross-stitches.

Bead Attachment

Use one strand floss to secure beads. Bring beading needle up from back of work, leaving 2" length of thread hanging; do not knot (end will be secured between stitches as you work). Thread bead on needle; complete stitch.

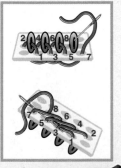

Do not skip over more than two stitches or spaces without first securing thread, or last bead will be loose. To secure, weave thread into several stitches on back of work. Follow graph to work design, using one bead per stitch.

Before You Begin

Assemble fabric, floss, pattern and tools. Familiarize yourself with the graph, color key and instructions before beginning.

Preparing Fabric

Before you stitch, decide how large to cut fabric. If you are making a pillow or other design which requires a large unstitched area, be sure to leave plenty of fabric. If you are making a small project, leave at least 3" around all edges of design. Determine the design area size by using this formula: number of stitches across design area divided by the number of threads per inch of fabric equals size of fabric in inches. Measure fabric, then cut evenly along horizontal and vertical threads.

Press out folds. To prevent raveling, hand overcast or machine zigzag fabric edges. Find center of fabric by folding horizontally and vertically, and mark with a small stitch.

Reading Graphs

Cross-stitch graphs or charts are made up of colors and symbols to tell you the exact color, type and placement of each stitch. Each square represents the area for one complete cross-stitch. Next to each graph, there is a key with information about stitches and floss colors represented by the graph's colors and symbols.

Color keys have abbreviated headings for cross-stitch (x), one-half cross-stitch (½x), quarter cross-stitch (¼x), three-quarter cross-stitch (¾x), backstitch (B'st), French knot (Fr), lazy daisy stitch (LzD) and straight stitch (Str). Some graphs are so large they must be divided for printing.

Preparing Floss

The six strands of floss are easily separated, and the number of strands used is given in instructions. Cut strands in 14"-18" lengths. When separating floss, always separate all six strands, then recombine the number of strands needed. To make floss separating easier, run cut length across a damp sponge. To prevent floss from tangling, run cut length through a fabric-softener dryer sheet before separating and threading needle. To colorfast red floss tones, which sometimes bleed, hold floss under running water until water runs clear. Allow to air dry.

X	B'st	Fr	DMC®	ANCHOR®	COLORS
			#307	#289	Lemon
			#310	#403	Black
			#433	#358	Med. Brown
			#435	#1046	Very Lt. Brown
			#437	#362	Lt. Tan
			#644	#830	Med. Beige Gray
			#645	#273	Very Dk. Beaver Gray
			#647	#1040	Med. Beaver Gray
			#676	#891	Lt. Old Gold
			#677	#886	Very Lt. Old Gold
			#700	#228	Bright Green
			#702	#226	Kelly Green
			#704	#256	Bright Chartreuse
			#725	#305	Topaz
			#727	#293	Very Lt. Topaz
			#729	#890	Med. Old Gold
			#776	#24	Med. Pink
			#818	#23	Baby Pink
			#822	#390	Lt. Beige Gray
			#899	#52	Med. Rose
			#3032	#903	Med. Mocha Brown
			#3033	#391	Very Lt. Mocha Brown
			#3045	#888	Dk. Yellow Beige
			#3046	#887	Med. Yellow Beige
			#3047	#852	Lt. Yellow Beige
			#3072	#847	Very Lt. Beaver Gray
			#3345	#268	Dk. Hunter Green
			#3348	#264	Lt. Yellow Green
			#3781	#1050	Dk. Mocha Brown
			#3799	#236	Very Dk. Pewter Gray
			White	#2	White

Stitching Techniques

Beginning & Ending a Thread

Try these methods for beginning a thread, then decide which one is best for you.

1: *Securing the thread*: Start by pulling needle through fabric back to front, leaving about 1" behind fabric. Hold this end with fingers as you begin stitching, and work over end with your first few stitches. After work is in progress, weave end through the back of a few stitches.

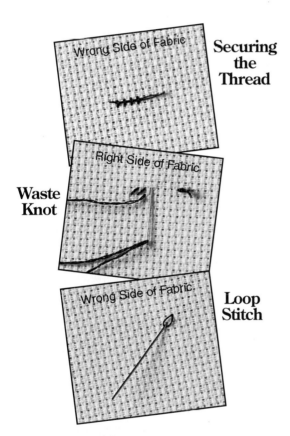

Securing the Thread

Wrong Side of Fabric

Right Side of Fabric

Waste Knot

Wrong Side of Fabric

Loop Stitch

2: *Waste knot*: Make a knot in end of floss and pull needle through fabric front to back several squares over from where your first cross-stitch will be. Come up at first stitch and stitch first few stitches over floss end. Clip knot.

3: *Loop stitch*: This method can only be used for even numbers of strands. Cut strands twice the normal length, then take half the number of strands needed and fold in half. Insert loose ends in needle and bring needle up from back at first stitch, leaving loop underneath. Take needle down through fabric and through loop; pull to secure.

For even stitches, keep a consistent tension on your thread, and pull thread and needle completely through fabric with each stab of the needle. Make all the top crosses on your cross-stitches face the same direction. To finish a thread, run the needle under the back side of several stitches and clip. Threads carried across the back of unworked areas may show through to the front, so do not carry threads.

Master Stitchery

Work will be neater if you always try to make each stitch by coming up in an unoccupied hole and going down in an occupied hole.

The sewing method is preferred for stitching on linen and some other evenweaves, but can also be used on Aida. Stitches are made as in hand sewing with needle going from front to back to front of fabric in one motion. All work is done from the front of the fabric. When stitching with the sewing

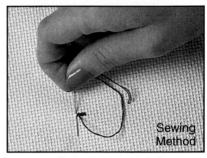

Sewing Method

method, it is important not to pull thread too tightly or stitches will become distorted. Stitching on linen is prettiest with the sewing method, using no hoop. If you use a hoop or frame when using the sewing method with Aida, keep in mind that fabric cannot be pulled taut. There must be "give" in the fabric in order for needle to slip in and out easily.

In the stab method, needle and floss are taken completely through fabric twice with each stitch. For

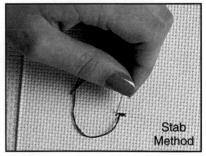

Stab Method

the first half of the stitch, bring needle up and pull thread completely through fabric to the front. Then take needle down and reach underneath and pull completely through to bottom.

Working on Evenweave

When working on linen or other evenweave fabric, keep needle on right side of fabric, taking needle front to back to front with each stitch. Work

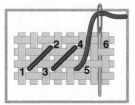

over two threads, placing the beginning and end of the bottom half of the first Cross-Stitch where a vertical thread crosses a horizontal thread.

Cleaning Your Needlework

Careful washing, pressing and sometimes blocking help preserve and protect your stitched piece. After stitching is complete, a gentle washing will remove surface dirt, hoop marks and hand oils that have accumulated on your fabric while stitching. Even if a piece looks clean, it's always a good idea to give it a nice cleaning before finishing. Never press your work before cleaning, as this only serves to set those hoop marks and soils that are best removed.

Using a gentle soap such as baby shampoo or gentle white dishwashing liquid and a large, clean bowl, make a solution of cool, sudsy water. If you use a handwash product, make sure the one you choose contains no chlorine bleach. Fill another bowl or sink with plain cool water for rinsing.

Soak your stitched piece in sudsy water for five to ten minutes. Then gently and without rubbing or twisting, squeeze suds through fabric several times. Dip piece several times in fresh cool water until no suds remain.

On rare occasions floss colors will run or fade slightly. When this happens, continue to rinse in cool water until water becomes perfectly clear. Remove fabric from water and lay on a soft, white towel. Never twist or wring your work. Blot excess water away and roll the piece up in the towel, pressing gently.

Never allow a freshly washed piece of embroidery to air dry. Instead, remove the damp piece from the towel and place face down on a fresh, dry white towel. To prevent color stains, it's important to keep the stitched piece flat, not allowing stitched areas to touch each other or other areas of the fabric. Make sure the edges of fabric are in straight lines and even. To be sure fabric edges are straight when pressing dry, use a ruler or T-square to check edges. Wash towel several times before using it to block cross-stitch, and use it only for this purpose.

After edges are aligned and fabric is perfectly smooth, cover the back of the stitched piece with a pressing cloth, cotton diaper or other lightweight white cotton cloth. Press dry with a dry iron set on a high permanent press or cotton setting, depending on fabric content. Allow stitchery to lie in this position several hours. Machine drying is acceptable after use for items like towels and kitchen accessories, but your work will be prettier and smoother if you give these items a careful pressing the first time.

Framing and Mounting

Shopping for Frames

When you shop for a frame, take the stitchery along with you and compare several frame and mat styles. Keep in mind the "feeling" of your stitched piece when choosing a frame. For example, an exquisite damask piece stitched with metallics and silk threads might need an ornate gold frame, while a primitive sampler stitched on dirty linen with flower thread would need a simpler, perhaps wooden frame.

Mounting

Cross-stitch pieces can be mounted on mat board, white cardboard, special padded or unpadded mounting boards designed specifically for needlework, or special acid-free mat board available from art supply stores. Acid-free framing materials are the best choice for projects you wish to keep well-preserved for future generations. If you prefer a padded look, cut quilt batting to fit mounting board.

Center blocked stitchery over mounting board of choice with quilt batting between, if desired. Leaving 1½" to 3" around all edges, trim excess fabric away along straight grain.

Mounting boards made for needlework have self-stick surfaces and require no pins. When using these products, lift and smooth needlework onto board until work is taut and edges are smooth and even. Turn board face down and smooth fabric to back, mitering corners.

Pins are required for other mounting boards. With design face up, keeping fabric straight and taut, insert a pin through fabric and edge of mounting board at the center of each side. Turn piece face down and smooth excess fabric to back, mitering corners.

There are several methods for securing fabric edges. Edges may be glued to mat board with liquid fabric glue or fabric glue stick. If mat board is thick, fabric may be stapled.

Mats & Glass

Pre-cut mats are available in many sizes and colors to fit standard-size frames. Custom mats are available in an even wider variety of colors, textures and materials. Using glass over cross-stitch is a matter of personal preference, but is generally discouraged. Moisture can collect behind glass and rest on fabric, causing mildew stains. A single or double mat will hold glass away from fabric.

Basic Stitchery

Cross-Stitch (x):

There are two ways of making a basic Cross-Stitch. The first method is used when working rows of stitches in the same color. The first

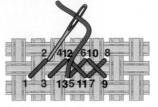

step makes the bottom half of the stitches across the row, and the second step makes the top half.

The second method is used when making single stitches. The bottom and top halves of each stitch are worked before starting the next stitch.

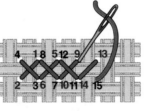

Quarter Cross-Stitch (¼x):

Stitch may slant in any direction.

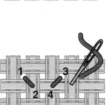

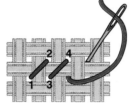

Half Cross-Stitch (½x):

The first part of a Cross-Stitch. May slant in either direction.

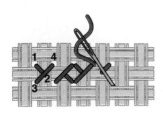

Three-Quarter Cross-Stitch (¾x): A

Half Cross-Stitch plus a Quarter Cross-Stitch. May slant in any direction.

Overcast:

is used to finish edges. Stitch two or three times in corners for complete coverage.

Embellishing with Embroidery

EMBROIDERY stitches add detail and dimension to stitching. Unless otherwise noted, work Backstitches first, then other embroidery stitches.

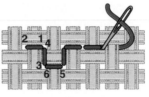

Straight Stitch

Lazy Daisy Stitch

Backstitch

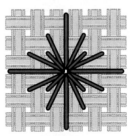

Modified Eyelet

French Knot

Bead Attachment Illustration

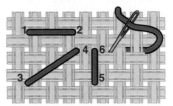

Use one strand floss to secure beads. Work all stitches in the same direction so beads will lie properly. Bring beading needle up from back of work, leaving 2" length of thread hanging; do not knot (end will be secured between stitches as you work). Thread bead on needle; complete stitch.

Do not skip over more than two stitches or spaces without first securing thread, or last bead will be loose. To secure, weave thread into several stitches on back of work. Follow graph to work design, using one bead per stitch.

Acknowledgments

Alice Peterson Co.
Stitch & Zip™ Cross Stitch Purse: Sunflower

Anne Brinkley from Thistle Needleworks, Inc.
Porcelain Box: Sunflower Bouquet

Charles Craft, Inc.
Aida: Balloon Fair; Hot Cocoa; Irish at Heart; Let it Rain; Nest for Rent; Pumpkin Patch; Rabbit in the Garden; Room for Love; Welcome
Cross Stitch Tote Bag: Crafty Keeper
Fiddler's Cloth: Old Quilts
Linen: Centuries of Santa
Royal Classic: Country Kitchen
Showcase Towels: Country-Time Towels

Coats & Clark
Anchor® Floss: Hot Cocoa; Room for Love
Braided Piping: Set Sail; Welcome

CPE, Inc.
Felt: Christmas Trims

Creative Beginnings
Charms: Teddy Bears in the Attic

Daniel Enterprise
Crafter's Pride Stitch-A-Mugs: Halloween Mugs
Napkin Ring: Country Kitchen
Vinyl-Aida™: Irish at Heart

Darice®
2 mm Chain: Teddy Bears in the Attic
Jingle Bells: Teddy Bears in the Attic
Ribbon Roses: Teddy Bears in the Attic

Deco Art™
Spray Varnish: Home on the Farm

DMC®
Broder Médici: Teddy Bears in the Attic
Embroidery Floss: All Things Grow; Balloon Fair; Be Mine; Centuries of Santa; Christmas Trims; Country Kitchen; Country-Time Towels; Crafty Keeper; Dutch Memories; Easter; Floral Fantasy; Floral Wreath; Flowers in the Kitchen; Fruit Stand; Garden Visions; Halloween Mugs; Haunted House; Holiday Reflections; Home on the Farm; Hot Cocoa; Irish at Heart; Ladybugs; Merry Christmas Stocking; Merry Santa; Ming Vases; Owls; Poinsettia; Pumpkin Patch; Roses and Lattice; Roses are Red; Seasons; Set Sail; Spooked; Springtime Stroll; Sunflower Bouquet; Teddy Bears in the Attic; Tiger Territory; Tulips; Welcome; Winter Skating; Wolves

Kreinik
Blending Filament: Hot Cocoa

La Mode
Buttons: Teddy Bears in the Attic

M.C.G. Textiles, Inc.
Afghan Cloth: Roses and Lattice

Mill Hill from Gay Bowles Sales, Inc.
Seed Beads: Merry Santa; Teddy Bears in the Attic
Stitchband: Ladybugs

Rainbow™ by Kunin Felt
Felt: Christmas Trims

Rainbow Gallery®
Wisper Floss: Merry Santa

Stitch-A-Blouse by Rushwear
Baby Bunting: Pumpkin Patch
Girls Blouse: Pumpkin Patch

Sudberry House
Classic Round Stool: Floral Wreath
Coasters: Fruit Stand
Horizontal Design Mirror: Winter Skating
Large Candle Screen: Holiday Reflections
Medium Tea Tray: Old Quilts
Petite Table: Ming Vases
Petite Tray: Fruit Stand
Royal Crown Plate: Poinsettia
Sharon's Box: Winter Skating
Small Tea Tray: Irish at Heart

Walnut Hollow
Basswood Country Plank: Owls
Made for Kids Hat Rack: Welcome
Picket Shelf: Nest for Rent

Wichelt Imports, Inc.
Aida: All Things Grow; Christmas Trims; Floral Coasters; Fruit Stand; Merry Santa; Set Sail; Wolves
Heart Shaped Bell Pull: Room for Love
Jobelan®: Flowers in the Kitchen; Seasons; Spooked; Tulips
Melinda: Sunflower Bouquet
Silk Linen: Poinsettia

Zweigart®
Aida: Be Mine; Haunted House; Merry Christmas Stocking
Cashel Linen: Home on the Farm
Dublin Linen: Ming Vases
Jubilee: Easter; Floral Fantasy; Garden Visions
Lugana®: Dutch Memories; Floral Wreath; Garden Visions; Owls; Tiger Territory
Meran: Winter Skating
Quaker Cloth: Roses are Red
Rustico Aida: Welcome Guest
Tabby Cloth: Springtime Stroll
Valerie: Holiday Reflections

Pattern Index

Designer Index